ADVANCE PRAISE

Human nature being as it is, and human societies being as they are, there is never a time or place when prophetic voices inherent dignity and radical equality of the human family is out of witness is sorely lacking and desperately hearted to read Charles Camosy *Losing Our Dignity: How Secularized Medicine Is Undermining Fundamental Human Equality*. Professor Camosy gives us what the Greeks called *parrhesia*—blunt speech, plain talk, bold truth-telling—about the consequences of abandoning a principle that is foundational to any sound account of medical ethics.

> **Robert P. George**, McCormick Professor of Jurisprudence, Princeton University

We are on the brink of a great precipice concerning human rights— do all persons matter equally because of who they are as members of the human family? Charles C. Camosy's powerfully insightful book explores one reason why some members of society have fallen out of our moral sphere of concern—the rise of secularized medicine and its view that only certain members of the human family are truly worth saving. Using poignant examples, Dr. Camosy issues a heart-felt call for us to find a path forward that reclaims an anthropology in which human beings are viewed as inherently valuable because they are the image bearers of God.

> **Kristin M. Collier**, MD, FACP, Assistant Professor of Internal Medicine and Director, The University of Michigan Medical School Program on Health, Spirituality and Religion

Charles Camosy is one of the most important Christian ethicists of our cultural moment, and *Losing Our Dignity* shows why. He sounds an alarm about changes in the medical culture of the West, which inevitably result in the victimization of the most vulnerable members of the human family. Camosy matches his urgent, dire diagnosis with a stirring vision of how individuals, families, and churches can resist our "throwaway culture." This book should be read by anyone with loved ones facing end-of-life concerns and anyone who longs to see a consistent pro-life ethic enacted in civil society and culture more generally.

Tish Harrison Warren, Anglican Priest and author of *Liturgy of the Ordinary* and *Prayer in the Night*

Charles Camosy's newest book makes a vital contribution to our understanding of health care in the United States. *"This book sounds a cultural alarm about these trends, especially with regard to key stages at which whole populations have lost their fundamental equality."* I witnessed this first hand when my mother, on more than one occasion, fearlessly advocated for my grandmother and other residents who had no one to advocate for them in a substandard "nursing home" in my home town. All people of good will should carefully weigh Camosy's message, and Catholic leaders in particular should read with urgency his call to action. I plan to share the book widely in my diocese and I hope others will as well.

The Most Reverend Kevin W. Vann, Bishop of Orange, CA

In a comprehensive and engaging way, Dr. Camosy continues to build the conversation framework for a consistent life ethic in which the inherent value and dignity of every human being is viewed through both scientific and philosophical lenses. As an occupational therapist, I can attest to the challenges facing healthcare practitioners today when our guidelines and practice standards do not align with patient needs or meaningful care. *Losing Our Dignity* uncovers inconsistencies in the way we deliver care and also provides an insightful warning: we risk losing our empathy, our connection, and our purpose if we continue turning a blind eye to relativistic policies and practices that undermine our dignity and a consistent respect for all life. Working with and caring for another person in a vulnerable state is a duty and a privilege. In addition to advancing the dialogue around a consistent life ethic globally, the Church must also continue our history of innovation in healthcare and answer the call to reimagine holistic service to others, especially the sick, fragile, or dying.

Erin Youkins Director of the Office of Life, Justice and Peace, Archdiocese of Baltimore

LOSING
OUR DIGNITY

How Secularized Medicine
Is Undermining Fundamental
Human Equality

CHARLES C. CAMOSY

New City Press
Hyde Park, New York

Published by New City Press
202 Comforter Blvd.,
Hyde Park, NY 12538
www.newcitypress.com

©2021 New City Press

2nd Printing, July 2022

Unless otherwise noted, all biblical quotations are from the
New Revised Standard Version Bible, copyright © 1989 National
Council of the Churches of Christ in the United States of America.

Losing Our Dignity
How Secularized Medicine Is Undermining
Fundamental Human Equality
Charles C. Camosy

Library of Congress Control Number: 2021934463

ISBN 978-1-56548-471-9 (paperback)
ISBN 978-1-56548-472-6 (e-book)
Printed in the United States of America

Contents

To my parents, Mary Ann and Raymond James,
who raised me (by both instruction and example)
to see the same image and likeness of God
in every single human being.

Preface and Acknowledgments

Some books have unclear beginnings, but that is not the case with this project. It was born of a single conversation with Bria Sandford at a coffee shop in the Bronx's Little Italy. Given how happy I am with where it ended up, I can't thank her enough for helping me begin this journey.

The project did take some twists and turns, especially as I educated myself on the realities of how we care for people with dementia. On this score, insights from Wendy Perry, Gil Atanasoff, Erin Younkins, Paula Taliaferro, and Julian Hughes were absolutely essential. Significant, too, were the insights into how the Focolare community responds to and seeks unity with their members who develop dementia— particularly the insights of Sue Kopp, Flavio Pedroni, and Susanne Janssen.

The pandemic gave new urgency to this project, especially as the stories of how people with dementia and other disabilities were being treated in nursing homes and other long-term care facilities came to light. I want to thank Shannon Bream and Tucker Carlson for having me on their cable news shows to discuss this, not least because of the mountain of messages I received afterward from concerned family members detailing their horrific realities. These real-life reminders that fundamental human equality was under attack served as intense motivation to finish the project with a sense of urgency.

Several people helped out by looking at a key chapter here or providing an essential insight on a particular problem there. Among them were Michael Peppard, Robert Troug, Bobby Schindler, Elizabeth R. Schiltz, Bo Bonner, and Carter Snead. I'm particularly grateful to those who read full versions of the manuscript at various points in the process and gave me critical feedback. These include Kristin Collier, Joe Vukov, Stephen Little, and Alexandra DeSanctis. My graduate assistants at Fordham, Carleton Chase and Jack Papas, were also quite helpful to me at various points.

Most importantly, I want to thank the wonderful people at New City Press for once again giving me the opportunity to publish with them. Here I must single out the indefatigable Tom Masters for a masterful edit, one deeply attuned to the spirituality of unity, which has made this a much better book. I look forward to many more years of working with them, God willing.

Can Fundamental Human Equality Survive Secularized Medicine?

Take a moment to think about people in your extended family and other social circles. It may not come to our conscious attention very often, but I suspect most of us have encountered a wide range of human difference, especially when it comes to neurological diversity. An uncle braving Alzheimer's disease. A cousin's prematurely-born child fighting for her life in the bed of a neonatal intensive care unit. A neighbor and war veteran suffering mental illness from post-traumatic stress disorder. A daughter's genius classmate who is off to college next year at age fifteen. A ridiculously happy younger brother with Down syndrome. The list of examples could be nearly endless.

We think even less often, I suspect, about what makes all these different kinds of human beings equal. By "equal" I'm not referring to sameness with regard to merely accidental traits, like how high they can jump or how powerful their memory is. No, here I am invoking what makes these human beings *fundamentally* equal to one another and to all human beings in their very essence. Being prompted to consider such a topic may seem strange, even offensive. Many of us rightly believe that a minimally decent culture must be based on fundamental human equality. Most of the Western world operates as if it is obvious that all human beings have it, even if we sometimes disagree about what such equality means. Indeed, this may be the great moral insight of Western culture, held by an overwhelming majority across a range of political affiliations and tribes.

But many secular[1] philosophers and other thinkers have struggled to come up with a sound basis for this kind of fundamental human equality. The theistic founders of the United States assumed that their audience would overwhelmingly agree that it is "self-evident" that all humans are created equal in dignity by God.[2] But that is no longer the case for many who hold power over life and death in the Western world. In our post-Christian culture, especially (but not only) among some in medicine whose opinions are authoritative and influential, a focus on levels of ability relative to one's autonomous will, self-awareness, rationality, productivity (especially as understood by a consumer culture that worships buying and selling), moral capacity, communication, and the like have led some to notice that not all human beings have these abilities in equal measure.[3] Indeed, some fellow members of the species *Homo sapiens* do not appear to have them at all. This helps explain why some of these thinkers have made a distinction between "human beings" and "persons." In this view, persons (that is, those who exhibit the kind of relevant abilities just mentioned) are indeed all equal. But not all human beings are equal. And not only that: in this view, certain human beings who are deemed non-persons may be classified as mere objects and discarded or even killed without significant moral or legal concern.[4]

Now, those who uphold fundamental human equality might dismiss the person vs. human being distinction as coming out of an academic fantasyland that very few who live in the real world believe in. I am sympathetic to the spirit of this critique, especially in other contexts, but in this case it doesn't apply. Particularly in the last fifty years or so, these ideas have made their way from the academic ivory tower into mainstream medical ethics and mainstream medicine. And given the authority and power medicine has had in the broader culture—especially about sacred matters of life and death—this book will focus on how such authority and power have put an increasing number of human beings outside the circle of protection based on fundamental equality.

This exclusion is happening largely without anyone realizing that rejecting Christian theology (and similar views held in Judaism and Islam) as the foundation of values undergirding our public policies has put fundamental human equality at risk. Yes, the founders of what would become the United States—especially given how they treated women and Blacks—failed to live out their belief in God-given human dignity and fundamental equality. But the ideal was never abandoned, and subsequent generations tried to live out the Christian ideal of equality more consistently.

This problem of inconsistency is not, obviously, unique to the US founders. Much of Christendom betrayed its own principles in this regard, especially via colonization of the so-called "New World." However, it was a Christian theology of universalism—focused on fundamental human equality—that ended up becoming the basis of the critiquing forces which eventually won the day. Here I have in mind the views associated with sixteenth-century Dominican missionary friars Antón Montesino and Bartolomé de las Casas. In response to members of their Church (and even their own order) who argued in favor of exploiting the native peoples of the New World, these friars castigated their fellow Christians using appeals to fundamental human equality. Montesino, for instance, delivered this astonishing sermon to a crowded church in Santo Domingo, Dominican Republic, on the Fourth Sunday of Advent in 1511:

> You are all in mortal sin. You live in it, you die in it. All because of the cruel tyranny you exercise against these innocent peoples. Tell me, by what right and with what justice do you so violently enslave these Indians? By what authority do you wage such hideous wars against these people who peacefully inhabit their lands, killing them by unspeakable means? How can you oppress them, giving neither food nor medicine and by working them to death, all for your insatiable thirst for gold? And what care are you providing them spiritually in teaching them about their God and creator, so they are baptized, hear Mass, and keep holy days? Are they not human beings? Do they not have rational souls? Are you not obligated to love them as you love yourselves?

Notre Dame moral theologian David Lantigua points out that the universalism these Spanish Dominicans defended went on to serve as the foundation for what in the West would eventually be called universal human rights.[5] Even secular giants like the philosopher Jürgen Habermas have come to appreciate the unique role Christian thought has played in what he called "egalitarian universalism." There is no alternative to Christianity, says Habermas, upon which to ground our contemporary notion of universal human rights.[6]

But over the last half-century something has changed. Contemporary Western culture has surrendered this deeply theological legacy more generally, but the surrender is especially advanced in a secularized and even irreligious understanding of medicine and health care.[7] This has put fundamental human equality at risk. Indeed, if we continue on our current path—if we cannot find a way to recover this legacy—the idea of fundamental human equality may simply die out. The damage already done has had disastrous consequences for some of the most vulnerable human beings among us, but this book will show that our rejection of human equality is on the verge of claiming a new, large, and growing set of victims: human beings with late-stage dementia. Indeed, the COVID-19 pandemic has revealed that a large-scale marginalization of this disabled population may already be underway.

This book sounds a cultural alarm about these trends, especially with regard to key stages at which whole populations have lost their fundamental equality. It will do so by focusing first on the stories of individuals put at risk by our rejection of fundamental human equality and then connect their stories to broader historical developments and ethical arguments.

Chapter 1 begins by demonstrating how contemporary Western health care owes its existence to religious (and especially Christian) institutions and ideas. It then shows how a secularized medical culture developed and how this culture affects our foundational moral views, with a particular focus on its rejection of the equality of all fellow human beings in favor of the equality of persons with traits like autonomy, rationality, and self-awareness. It will also show how, in recent years, the culture of medicine and medical ethics has become intentionally and openly hostile to religious ideas and theological perspectives. It will finish by concluding that, though this culture imagines or pretends to be neutral, the debate over human vs. personal equality cannot take place in an imagined secularized nowhere. Religious and spiritual views must be engaged on the same playing field as secular views of what is ultimately true and good.

The next several chapters of the book focus on key medical developments over the last half-century, with attention to their impact on particularly vulnerable human beings. Chapter 2 begins with the story of Jahi McMath and the debate over living human beings with dead (or mostly-dead) brains. Chapter 3 tells the story of Terri Schiavo and the interesting new debate over human beings deemed to be in a vegetative state. Chapter 4 focuses on the story of the "Roe baby," who prompted the landmark US Supreme Court case on abortion, *Roe v. Wade*. Chapter 5 examines the story of Alfie Evans and the contemporary debate over the moral and legal standing of babies and toddlers with neurodegenerative disease.

Chapter 6 tells multiple stories about the future victims of the cultural rejection of human equality if we stay on this terrible course—with a particular focus on human beings who have late-stage dementia. Because they frequently are no longer autonomous, self-aware, productive (again, especially from the perspective of consumer culture), or rational, they no longer have the traits of persons as defined by a secularized medical (and legal) establishment. It is therefore only a matter of time before we follow our principles where they lead and deem these people (and likely others with profound mental disabilities) to be human non-persons as well. The pressure to do this will be especially intense in the coming years because—as is the case to one degree or another in all of the stories just mentioned—adequately respecting the full and equal dignity of these human beings requires addressing the problem of scarce medical resources. Especially in a consumer culture which encourages us to live ever more "productive" lives, will we spend these resources on human beings who for all the world look like they fail contemporary tests for personhood? The pressure will be high to avoid allocating these resources to such populations, especially as (1) fiscal indebtedness puts massive pressure on national health-care budgets and (2) baby boomers and Generation X continue to age and many millions more are faced with very expensive dementia care.[8]

Many traditionally religious people are already quite aware of the victims produced by this rejection of fundamental human equality and worry about those who may be next. But they are also quite aware that, if this powerful secularizing influence cannot be reversed, intentional religious communities (a paradigmatic example might be the Little Sisters of the Poor) who welcome these vulnerable human beings into the intimate spaces of their lives can and will provide a bulwark against these practices. This book concludes with stories of international religious communities from ages past that provide hopeful models for our own cultural moment.

But just before that, chapter 7 calls for dialogue with those who are not as comfortable with traditional religious ideas—or at least not as comfortable placing them at the foundation of our cultural values and legal protections. The dialogue I propose appeals to the sensibilities of secular progressives with respect to social equality and social justice as a way of bridging a gap with religious traditionalists. I suggest that this dialogue highlights a common goal: resisting our consumerist tendency to rate the value of human beings based on what they can produce or on their level of ability, often in "ableist" ways which discriminate against the disabled, presuming their lives and contributions to be inferior. Such a dialogue would bring forward areas in our shared visions of the good (even if it will not be perfectly realized) which suggest that all human beings must be recognized as morally and legally equal regardless of what they can do, whether or not they happen to be autonomous, and whether or not they are considered productive members of society. If that dialogue does not bring results (or takes longer than a decade or so to produce them), however, I argue that traditional religious communities (local congregations as well as vowed religious orders) must band together to care for these vulnerable human beings in a sign of opposition to a culture that has rejected their fundamental human equality. Indeed, if the past is any guide, new religious orders will rise up (and current ones will reorient themselves) to meet the need posed by this new threat.

But it is difficult to see how religious institutions alone—at least without some kind of larger cultural religious revival—could meet the prodigious levels of need if those with late-stage dementia are abandoned by the broader culture. In order to maximize the chances of success in meeting the coming challenge, we must reclaim a vision that considers the most vulnerable human beings as the moral and legal equals of those who have power over them. It is a particular challenge when so many of those with such power have largely rejected the central theological idea behind the vision: that fellow members of the species *Homo sapiens* share a dignified nature in common. Our dignity comes from a common nature that bears the image and likeness of God.[9] Because every living human being shares this dignified nature—regardless of age, level of ability, disease, etc.—we can speak about equality.

Can those who hold different theological and philosophical understandings still coalesce around a vision of the good that reasserts fundamental human equality? I think there are reasons for hope, but we obviously don't know yet. Here is one thing we do know: for decades now a poison, one that is fatal to fundamental human equality, has been spreading throughout our most powerful cultural and medical institutions. That poison is a new kind of secularity, one that is hostile to the theological ideas undergirding fundamental human equality. The antidote requires dialogue that is at least open to (and perhaps even willing to embrace) traditional religious views about the God-given human nature we all share. Because medical culture is uniquely responsible for so much of the damage, it must lead the way by engaging in cultural reforms that protect fundamental human equality. Happily, not only is this possible, but in some contexts the antidote has already been administered and the healing already begun.

Chapter One

The Secularization of Medicine and Medical Ethics

Deep Connections between Medicine and Religion

For most of human history, the practice of healing and the practice of religious faith were closely connected. Often the healer and the religious figure were the same person. In fact, despite the hard separation between the two in the developed West, the historical connection is so strong that contemporary secularized medicine retains vestiges of religiosity, for instance, in the training for and practice of health care. Physicians, distinguished in their special white coats, are endowed with the bearing and cultural authority of a modern-day shaman or priest. Contemporary ceremonies at which medical students first receive their white coats—and, later on, formally recite a (properly adapted, of course) version of the Hippocratic Oath—resemble religious liturgies or priestly ordinations.[10] The near complete privacy attached to the physician-patient relationship resembles the seal of the confessional, where a priest may not share what a person reveals in the sacrament. The authority of medical science—although under threat in some quarters—is still one of the closest things we have to a secular Delphic oracle. During the COVID-

19 pandemic, for instance, titles like "physician," "scientist," or "epidemiologist" were invoked as quasi-religious authorities. In public discourse, the most fatal accusation is that one's "anti-science" approach is blocking medicine's truth and progress.

In some ways this separation is obviously a good thing. Those who value real results for real people don't want a health care based on reading entrails or ritual sacrifice. But in other ways the separation is a significant problem. As we will see in more detail, a secularized (and hyper-specialized) culture can reduce caring for a patient's health merely to maintaining or fixing her organic plumbing, so to speak. This is an important part of health care, of course: several people I love are alive today because of these technical skills. But such skill, however impressive, has been largely and unnecessarily severed from something at least as important: treating the human person in the fullness of who she is, including her particular understanding of the good. And this requires considering the kinds of existential questions and ultimate concerns engaged by theology.

Christianity, in particular, shaped Western culture's understanding of medicine in this light—not least because the Gospel of Jesus Christ is chock full of healing stories. Consider, for example, the Gospel reading in the Roman Catholic liturgical calendar for the Third Sunday of Advent:

> When John heard in prison of the works of the Messiah, he sent his disciples to him with this question, "Are you the one who is to come, or should we look for another?" Jesus said to them in reply, "Go and tell John what you hear and

see: the blind regain their sight, the lame walk, the lepers are cleansed, the deaf hear, the dead are raised, and the poor have the good news proclaimed to them." (Mt 11:2-5, NABRE)

When pressed by disciples of John the Baptist to give an account of himself so they could determine whether he was the Messiah, the chosen one of God, Jesus did not speak of using his power to incite revolutions. Nor did he call for political change or invoke his regal status. Instead, he focused on the fact that sick people came to him for help—and were made whole. This is why Jesus is famously called "the great physician," for he directly and analo-gously thinks of his work in precisely these terms. Indeed, Mark chapter 2, Matthew chapter 9, and Luke chapter 5 relate the account of Jesus healing the paralytic (who, in two of the accounts, is dramatically lowered from a hole in the roof to circumvent the great crowd that had gath-ered) with the provocative words "your sins are forgiven." Later in the chapter, when Jesus is challenged to explain why he spends so much time with the outcasts of society (including the "untouchables" of the day, like lepers), he says, "Those who are well have no need of a physician, but those who are sick; I have come to call not the righteous but sinners" (Mk 2:17).

The early Church, unsurprisingly, took its cues from Jesus the Physician and centered much of its ministry on care of the sick and disabled—especially the untouch-able sick and disabled discarded by the dominant cul-ture. Rodney Stark, Distinguished Professor of the Social Sciences at Baylor University, has argued that such care spurred the improbable growth of a small religious sect into the official religion of the Roman Empire. In his 1996 book *The Rise of Christianity*, Stark argues that care for (and even adoption of) the sick, the disabled, and female infants typically exposed and left to die (or, if allowed to live, pressed into slavery or prostitution or both), along with a refusal to abandon the sick during plagues, made the Christian witness deeply attractive to converts.[11] His research, for instance, found that the Antonine plague (second century), the Cyprian plague (third century), and the Justinian plague (sixth century) led to significant increases in conversion rates to Christianity.

In the early Church, bishops and other wealthy or important Christians were expected to open their houses in hospitality to the sick. Eventually, especially after Christianity became an accepted religion in the fourth century, this practice led to the development of formal hospital and nursing facilities. A dramatic early instance is seen in the work of St. Ephrem, who, during a plague at Edessa in 375, provided hundreds of beds for the afflicted. But perhaps the most famous early example of a hospital is that of St. Basil of Caesarea in Cappadocia in 369. His facility "took on the dimensions of a city," boasting organized systems of streets, buildings for different kinds of patients, and even living spaces for physicians and nurses.[12]

The Rule of St. Benedict, written in the early fifth century, insisted that "care of the sick is to be placed above and before every other duty."[13] Andrew Crislip shows that many Christian monasteries focused so intensely on health care that they eventually and naturally became full-time hospitals.[14] Such values and practices among those who follow Jesus influenced Christendom during the Middle Ages, when the number of hospitals as well as schools for training physicians and nurses increased dramatically. Driven by a parallel increase in religious and military orders devoted to ministering to the sick, by the late Middle Ages "nearly every city" in Europe had a "hospital of the Holy Ghost," so named for the hospitals established by the Order of the Holy Ghost, which was founded in France.[15]

I myself have been doing research on nursing ethics, especially as seen in the history of nursing. By the end of the Middle Ages and into the early modern period, well-established orders of Catholic nuns had spread throughout Europe, precursors of what we call nurses today. For example, the Daughters of the Holy Spirit were founded in 1706 "to serve God by serving the poor, the sick, and the children."[16] The excellent and thorough care they provided included meeting medical as well as spiritual needs. Indeed, these sister-nurses were trained in their motherhouse to practice a wide variety of medicine, especially in rural settings where they weren't seen as competition for doctors. Tim McHugh's research on the Daughters' work in rural France reveals that they were taught "to diagnose, to prescribe treatment, and to prepare medications." Still-extant records of contracts show that these nuns considered "active medical intervention through the providing of remedies or through the services commonly offered by surgeons of equal importance as their nursing and spiritual consoling of the sick."[17]

Another significant group of sister-nurses were the Daughters of Charity of St. Vincent de Paul. In the mid-1800s, Sr. Matilda Coskery wrote *Advices Concerning the Sick*, the first comprehensive document on nursing. Significantly, these sisters saw their role as providing not only physical but also spiritual healing. Mother Mary Xavier Clark noted that when a sister leaves his bedside, a patient should be able to say, "That Sister is more like an angel than a human being. The very sight of her makes me think of God and love him."[18] Like the Daughters of the Holy Spirit who preceded them, the Daughters of Charity focused on the spiritual but were also expert in caring for their patients' physical bodies. Florence Nightingale's encounter with a nursing mission run by the Daughters of Charity in Alexandria, Egypt, deeply influenced her own journey toward nursing.

The French Revolution—and succeeding secularizing and anti-Catholic trends of the Enlightenment—led the Daughters of the Holy Spirit and the Daughters of Charity to move to the United States, where they were afforded religious freedom to pursue their ministry.[19] They joined several other orders of women religious who focused on nursing and health care, including the Sisters of Mercy, another group of sister-nurses who had a profound influence on Florence Nightingale. I will describe it in more detail in the conclusion to this book; for now, suffice it to say that the health-care infrastructure of the United States was built up by orders of women religious who came to North America during the mid-to-late nineteenth century. Sometimes, such as during an outbreak of cholera and typhoid in San Francisco, they had to build their own hospitals because the local government (in this case, the racist and anti-Catholic Know Nothings) forbade them from working in already-existing facilities. When the Spanish flu pandemic hit in the early twentieth century, these remarkable Catholic nuns sprang into action all over the world, serving in dramatic ways in the United States (particularly in Philadelphia[20]) especially. Such examples are models for mobilizations that we may well need again.

To this day an emphasis on health care lives most strongly in the Church. Indeed, the Catholic Church is the largest non-governmental provider of health care in the world. Catholic health-care facilities deliver about a quarter of health-care services worldwide.[21] In the United States alone, the Catholic Church operates nearly 700 hospitals and more than 1600 continuing care clinical facilities.[22] Remarkably, on a given day, one in seven US patients is served in a Catholic hospital. Catholic health care is so prevalent in the United States, including in poor areas with underserved populations, that some who disapprove of any influence of religion in medical care worry because Catholic institutions—and the values underpinning their work—are the only ones serving certain populations.[23]

Authentic Catholic approaches to health care (like the approach of Jesus himself) focus not only on the patients' organic structures, but also the good of the patients as persons in the fullness of who they are. For this reason, Catholic health-care clinics and training facilities have been at the forefront of medical ethics for centuries. In the Middle Ages, for instance, moral-theological debates—

such as whether refusing a life-saving amputation (without anesthetic, obviously) on the battlefield was the equivalent of suicide—led to the moral distinction between ordinary and extraordinary means of medical treatment. Indeed, in Western universities medical ethics first developed as a subdiscipline of Catholic moral theology. Although contemporary academic culture makes it nearly impossible to imagine, it is indisputable that the Catholic Church invented the field of medical ethics.[24]

A Shift toward Secularization and Irreligion

The 1970s was an era of fundamental change, including in medical ethics. Dan Callahan, who more than anyone else built the new version of the field, recalls the details in his memoir, *In Search of the Good: A Life in Bioethics*.[25] In the 1960s there were only a handful of philosophers engaging questions of medical ethics, but in just a few years it all changed. Callahan describes the philosophers as moving intentionally and quickly to "overshadow" and, eventually, simply to push aside the moral theologians. They did so by means of different language and concepts, sharply contrasting styles of argumentation, and (with some exceptions) a striking secular outlook and open hostility to religious ideas. The hostility between moral theologians and philosophers was so strong, Callahan notes, that when assembling bioethics research teams he spent much of his time managing the philosophers' anger because he invited theologians to participate.[26]

Callahan was fighting a losing battle. This secularizing philosophical approach came to dominate what was read and used in the field. Tom Beauchamp and James Childress's *Principles of Biomedical Ethics*, first published in 1979 (with an eighth edition published in 2019[27]), exemplifies this dominance. Theologians close to both Protestant and Catholic bioethics (like Joseph Fletcher, Paul Ramsey, Charles Curran, and Richard McCormick[28]) sometimes could not be distinguished from their secular counterparts because their perspectives included little or no explicit theological content. To remain at or near the top of the new discipline, or even merely to be welcome in it, they were forced to strip most of their theology out of their bioethical research.[29]

But those who advocated secularizing approaches were not content merely to dominate the field. The hostility toward theological bioethics became so strong that theological approaches became almost totally marginalized. For many years, the most important conference in the field—hosted by the American Society for Bioethics and Humanities (ASBH)—has become something close to hostile to proposals with explicitly theological arguments at their center. Theological proposals which present fundamental matters of metaphysics or ontology (rather than technocratic or procedural issues) are almost never accepted. Those of us in the field have recognized this clear hostility unfolding over the better part of a decade.[30]

Indeed, any doubt about the attitude toward theological approaches was put aside in December 2012 when philosopher Timothy Murphy's "In Defense of Irreligious Bioethics" was featured in the *American Journal of Bioethics* (AJOB).[31] Murphy's article, which has become widely influential,[32] argues that theologians and religious traditions involved in bioethics should face a "hermeneutic of suspicion." He claimed (with remarkable candor) that religious traditions should be singled out and repudiated. Indeed, he argued that such hostility "may even be morally required" of secular bioethicists. I say more about this in chapter 7, but it is worth noting that as this book goes to press, AJOB has published an issue (the target article of which argues for "re-establishing the relationship between theological and secular bioethics"[33]) which takes as its working assumption that Murphy's goals have been largely achieved.

And though AJOB and ASBH serve as flagships for the field, the examples cited above are but some dramatic examples of secularizing irreligion which have surfaced in recent years. A 2018 *BMJ* article from Richard Smith and Jane Blazerby, for instance, argued that in journal articles or other academic contexts religious belief ought to be declared as a "competing interest."[34] We will see more evidence below about how this kind of irreligious attitude has moved from medical ethics to the medical profession itself, but it is worth noting that an increasing number of applicants for medical residencies are being advised not to reveal, for instance, that they are members of the Catholic Medical Students Association or that they volunteer at their local church. In the judgment of these mentors, the discrimination they are likely to face for their religious commitments would outweigh any possible benefits of disclosing the information.[35]

Even when theologians tried to work with concepts and terms that had been evacuated of their theological content—as was the case with the rise in references to seemingly unobjectionable concepts like "human dignity"—the secular inquisition remained hostile, sensing something out of line. One clear example is that of Ruth Macklin, a well-known clinical bioethicist at Einstein Hospital in the Bronx, who wrote a scathing article titled "Dignity is a Useless Concept." In it she argued that the concept of human dignity can and should be removed from bioethics and replaced with "autonomy"—by which she means "a capacity for rational thought and action." This, she argued, could happen without any loss of content except, perhaps, for those who identify with "the many religious sources that refer to human dignity, especially but not exclusively in Roman Catholic writings."[36] Steven Pinker did her one better in his *New Republic* article "The Stupidity of Dignity." Here Pinker laid the problem even more directly at the feet of religious thought: he located the term "dignity" in "a movement to impose a radical political agenda, fed by fervent religious impulses, onto American biomedicine."[37]

It would be ethically questionable if, as Pinker worried, the religious invocation of human dignity were an attempt to impose an agenda upon those who thought differently. But the hostility toward religious approaches is now so ensconced in contemporary bioethics that those with the power to do so are seeking to quash the private views of individual religious conscience, even when those with such views do not attempt to impose anything onto anyone. Consider, for instance, what influential Canadian bioethicist Udo Schuklenk writes in the respected *Journal of Medical Ethics*, in an article titled "Professionalism

Eliminates Religion as a Proper Tool for Doctors Rendering Advice to Patients."[38] Here Schuklenk asserts that "professionalism" demands a physician check her foundational understandings of good at the door—even if a patient seeks out a health-care provider or institution precisely because the provider and the patient share the same or similar religious understanding of the good. Many irreligious philosophers are quite happy to impose, say, their particular brand of utilitarianism (despite it also being a particular understanding of the good) onto health-care providers and institutions that think differently. But they are also quite happy to single out particular understandings of the good—the ones they don't like—for marginalization.

Wesley Smith points out that if Schuklenk is correct about the role of religion in health care, it follows that he is also calling into question the very existence of Catholic and other religious hospitals (at least those motivated by their particular mission and identity in identifiable ways).[39] Schuklenk is joined by one of the most prominent bioethicists and physicians in the United States, Ezekiel Emanuel (one of the chief architects of the Affordable Care Act), who insists that those with religious views at odds with his understanding of the consensus in the secularized medical professions have only two choices: (1) choose an area of medicine which isn't impacted all that much by one's understanding of the good (he suggests radiology) or (2) don't get into medicine at all.[40] Schuklenk would facilitate this cultural change by barring people with religious views he doesn't like from medical, nursing, and pharmacy schools.[41]

Such hostile and hegemonic approaches to a genuine diversity of views about the good held by health-care providers already have produced real-world consequences— especially when agreed to by powerful secular-minded individuals in clinical medicine. A court in Ontario, Canada, for instance, recently found that physicians with moral objections to Canada's new assisted suicide law must either help patients die or "change . . . the nature of their practice if they intend to continue practicing medicine in Ontario."[42] Nurses in the United States who identify as religious pro-lifers are being forced (and even tricked[43]) into participating in the killing of prenatal children. For several years now the American Civil Liberties Union (ACLU) has been training its legal guns on Catholic hospitals that refuse to do certain kinds of abortions.[44] Even the *New England Journal of Medicine* has published articles arguing that Catholic hospitals should be forced to do abortions.[45]

The practice of medicine at one time was so connected to the Church and to Christian theology in the West, as we have seen, that the two could not be considered separately. But medicine is now dominated by secularized bioethics. Part of this influence can be explained by the deliberate attempt by the philosophers who took over bioethics, as Callahan notes, to be "on the firing line of ethics, working directly with the physicians"[46]; these philosophers reaped clear rewards for cultivating their on-the-ground influence. But medicine's own cultural move toward secularization, apart from the field of bioethics, is a very important part of the story of this chapter as well.

A Secularized Medical Culture

Jonathan Imber, the Glasscock Professor of Sociology at Wellesley College, has studied the decline of moral authority in contemporary medicine, at least for individual patients.[47] (The moral authority of medicine in politics, policy, and public discourse is another matter. As discussed above, that kind of authority has been largely unaffected.) In his book *Trusting Doctors: The Decline of Moral Authority in American Medicine*, Imber shows that, at least in the United States, individuals tended to trust medicine because of its religious foundations. When those foundations became unstable in the 1970s, trust in the medical profession suffered a similar fate. Here is just one of several examples he cites in the book: during the 1960s the American Medical Association maintained a vibrant cooperative relationship between religion and health care, but by the end of that decade the effort "lost its force" as the secularizing trends undermined that connection.

Patients can no longer count on practitioners of medicine to incorporate trust-building spiritual or religious aspects in their care, so they look for it elsewhere, including from hospital chaplains. This is what a wife and husband research team at Harvard Medical School, Tracy and Michael Balboni, found. Their recent book, *Hostility to Hospitality: Spirituality and Professional Socialization within Medicine*, provides essential insights on a number of topics. But perhaps most importantly, it confirms the centrality of spirituality and religion for patients—especially when facing existential questions about their health care. Their findings show clearly that illness "is a spiritual event," especially when the "cultural camouflage" around death and dying disappears.[48] In some ways, the Balbonis' marriage and work partnership (she's a physician, he's a theologian, and both are deeply committed Christians) exhibits the very thing they want to show: that those who want to provide patients the very best care can and should connect medicine and religion much more strongly.[49]

Unfortunately, their research also shows that, despite patients' strong desire for this connection, they do not experience it in contemporary medicine—even in offices seemingly geared toward meeting this need, like hospital chaplaincies. Significantly, these conclusions are based on their pioneering qualitative sociological work at the Harvard Initiative on Health, Religion, and Spirituality. They probed beyond mere numbers into individual patients' life stories. They also underline that the patients they consulted for their research came from a metro area (Boston) which is significantly more secular than other places in the United States. Unlike some research based on a biased sample size reflecting the views of the researchers, their results likely underreport the clear and unmet need for more spiritual care in US medicine.

The Balbonis' data show that both patients and providers clearly recognize the value of spiritual care. Furthermore, although physicians and nurses themselves are personally more religious than one might think, the data revealed a gap, an unmet need, facilitated by the culture of contemporary medicine. Specifically, they identify three interrelated facts about contemporary health care that currently make it "implausible" for religion and medicine to connect in a way that would better serve patients and better reflect the views of providers:[50]

- Hospitals are spaces set apart for advanced technological interventions and are largely understood to be places for curing, not for caring.

- As leaders of health-care teams, physicians have a derivative social authority to intervene in a person's life for their health which comes from the prior authority of the scientific method they employ.

- Contemporary medicine is often geared toward avoiding or forestalling death—which is at odds with a religious approach that emphasizes the reality of death and highlights the limitations of medicine to avoid or forestall it.

Indeed, they note that in the cultural imagination of contemporary medicine, religion has a place only when the medical arsenal has been exhausted and death is imminent. In this context, religion becomes strongly identified with death—so if the cultural camouflage surrounding it is to remain effective, religion must be kept on the margins until no other outcome is possible.

This explains, the Balbonis argue, why health-care providers do not offer spiritual care even when they personally understand its importance. Though this is often put down to a physician's lack of expertise in the subject matter, something more subtle and even subconscious is going on: medical teams are structured to act for the good of "temporal salvation." Contemporary medicine has limited itself to an "immanent frame" that focuses its attention completely on physical human flourishing. The social structures of contemporary medicine, after all, limit its authority to what the scientific method can support. In many medical contexts, explicit concern for the transcendent goods at stake, or even *acknowledging the possibility* that such goods should be engaged in a medical context, simply doesn't fit secularized medicine's understanding of itself.

Physicians being robbed by their own secularized culture of the chance to engage their patients (and to engage the practice of medicine itself) with explicit attention to these transcendent human goods in turn reduces human beings to mere organic machines. And the move in this direction has been accelerated as medicine continues to redefine itself in terms of specialties and subspecialties that do not focus on the fullness of a human being's reality, but on increasingly particular segments of a human being's organic structure and functioning.

Consider that a future physician's first real interaction with a human body as a subject of medical study is with a dead one. Jeff Bishop (a physician and Christian philosopher) argues that this first instance of training makes perfect sense, because this is how medicine overall is conceived in the contemporary West.[51] What future physicians learn in gross anatomy about specific organs, tubes, and systems is the beginning of socializing them to think about the nature of human reality as a series of organs, tubes, and systems. While in many circumstances this has produced better specialized care (and, again, many people I love are walking around alive today because of it), this shift has distanced Western medicine from considering the "final cause" of human beings—that is, from going beyond questions of merely how various aspects of the human body work to considering what human bodies are and what their purpose is. Thus, Bishop argues, contemporary medicine understands human beings as little more than anticipations of the corpses physicians first explored in medical school.

Why It Is Impossible to Practice Secularized Medicine

The terms *secular*, *secularized*, and *irreligious* have appeared several times already in this book—and in this section it may be important to go beyond "showing" how I'm using them and do a bit of "telling" as well. By a *secular* culture or discourse I have in mind one which, while welcoming people with religious beliefs, asks that they focus primarily on using an ethical language with terms and ideas that have no explicit religious content. Here I'm thinking of the bioethics culture and discourse into which theologians like McCormick, Ramsey, and Fletcher were integrated at the highest levels in the 1970s and '80s, but only if they translated their theological commitments out of their arguments and ideas, which were to be presented in the language demanded of them by those who held power in the field. By a *secularized* or *secularizing* culture or discourse I have in mind one which (sometimes unintentionally) cuts participants off from their source of faith and meaning for articulating and explicitly invoking the importance of transcendental goods, final causes, and ultimate concerns. A good example is the medical culture described by the

Balbonis: one which doesn't allow for discussion of these kinds of ideas even using secular language. Finally, by an *irreligious* culture or discourse I have in mind one which, with open and intentional hostility, seeks to repudiate and exclude ideas, people, and institutions which give off even a whiff of the religious or theological.

In some circumstances these categories may overlap, but in other circumstances it is important to keep them distinct. For instance, even if one takes an irreligious approach to medicine and medical ethics, I want to show in this section why it is impossible to practice a totally secularized medicine. While current practice generally avoids something like an explicit focus on transcendental goods, final causes, or ultimate concerns, such theological concepts nevertheless find their way into the design and practice of medicine in various ways. Indeed, it would be impossible to engage in any genuinely human endeavor without them—much less one so full of profound meaning as the practice of medicine. The Balbonis use the phrase "chief love" to name what medicine should engage more directly and honestly; but whatever words are used to name them, here's the bottom line: it is impossible to care for the health of a single human being (much less design and work within a health-care system with limited resources that must yet provide for millions) without incorporating such goods and values and purposes.

Indeed, even when proponents of secularization insist on excluding religion from their conceptual space, they nevertheless can't help but smuggle in *their* transcendental goods, final causes, ultimate concerns, or chief loves. For a good example, recall how Professor Schuklenk claimed that medicine must not make space for freedom of conscience for religious health-care providers. In that article he bemoaned the "sorts of doctors" who are willing to "prioritize their private beliefs, ultimately, over patient well-being."[52] If Professor Schuklenk is consistent—and not just singling out the private beliefs of people he doesn't like—then *all* private beliefs are going to be ruled out. But then how can a physician determine the well-being of her patients, except by using her private beliefs? Maybe it could be done if medicine were limited to the technical expertise involving organic plumbing and carpentry, but we have already seen how any practice geared toward the good of human beings must be much more than this.

Here are a few more examples to drive home the point. Suppose a physician believes that lying about the nature of a mass or nodule on a chest x-ray could produce a better consequence for her patient, a long-time smoker. Suppose her patient is in mental anguish for having a right leg that, because he strongly believes it does not belong there, requests that it be cut off, even though it is healthy. Suppose two of her needy, longtime patients (who have nowhere else to go to get good care) have bedbugs and her hospital administration is putting heavy pressure on her to drop them from her practice. Suppose a physically healthy eleven-year-old boy, who believes he was born in the wrong body, is requesting (against the will of his parents) that his healthy male sex organs be removed and replaced with nonfunctioning female ones. Suppose the most efficient non-human research we can do on cancer drugs requires us to create hundreds of mice with lethal cancer. Suppose parents ask to forgo life-sustaining treatment for their newborn daughter, not because the treatment isn't effective, but because their daughter has Down syndrome. Suppose parents who are insured by the state Medicaid program ask for five million dollars' worth of experimental treatment on their newborn son.

I could go on, but I trust the point has been made. What to do (or not do) in any of these situations requires thinking—and thinking hard—about one's particular ideas about what is ultimately true and good. By definition such ideas are not and cannot be taught in a medical textbook focused on the knowledge and skills needed to gain technical expertise. Becoming an excellent organic plumber or carpenter will not help you decide whether, say, your patients can demand activity from you that is not geared toward making a body healthier. Or whether patients must always be told the truth even when it may be easier for them to hear a falsehood. Or what kind of harm can be inflicted on non-human animals in the service of the health of human animals. Or whether the cleanliness of the hospital matters more than providing care to long-time and vulnerable patients. Or whether the good of an individual patient can be trumped by the good of the broader community.

Decisions about these matters can be made only on the basis of goods and values that transcend the immanent concerns on which Western medicine understands itself to be exclusively focused. It doesn't work to follow Professor Schuklenk in referring to "patient well-being" if we can't agree on what "well-being" means in a particular circumstance—much less in circumstances where there is dramatic public disagreement. Secular utilitarians, Muslim human rights activists, reproductive justice feminists, Catholic virtue ethicists, libertarian nationalists, Bible-focused Evangelicals, atheistic anarchists, Jewish casuists—that is, *everyone*—must bring their own particular understanding of the good to bear on these questions. There is simply no way to avoid it—or to avoid the profound cultural disagreement that comes with it.

Given my central concern in this project, I want to underline that this is very much the case when it comes to the discussion of the human being vs. the human person raised in the introduction. Some claim that we are "persons," with certain morally relevant actualized capacities, rather than human animals with a shared nature. This view comes from a particular understanding of the good. And, as the professors Balboni point out, such a view can come only from an implicitly theological perspective—even if the view is held by people without an explicitly religious orientation. One correct way to think about theology is as the study of what is fundamentally and ultimately true. Thus "theological" is a proper way to categorize a question about the fundamental and ultimate truth about who we are, even in a medical context—perhaps especially in a medical context.[53]

There is no neutral way to answer the fundamental question of who "we" ultimately are. False and misguided claims about the necessity of establishing a secularized and "neutral" space conceal particular and private visions of the good being smuggled into the judgments that are made.

Even more, they can be used as weapons to marginalize or exclude political adversaries with a different point of view. A secular activist for migrants' rights, for instance, generally won't exclude Pope Francis's activism in favor of the full cultural inclusion of migrants from our public discourse simply because of the pope's clear theological commitments. On the other hand, an abortion activist will often try to exclude St. John Paul II's thought concerning the full inclusion of prenatal children in our culture precisely because of the pope's clear theological commitments. The only fair way to approach the foundational question of who we are is for all of us, religious and secular, to acknowledge that we indeed all have ultimate concerns and transcendental values and that we must do our level best not to exclude anyone from public discourse simply because we don't like their point of view.

Over the past fifty years, as both medicine and medical ethics became secularized, the issue of human identity migrated from a question about our common humanity to one about traits and capacities we share in common. Beauchamp and Childress, both secular principlists, claimed to focus equally on four concepts: autonomy, non-maleficence, beneficence, and justice. But because there is no neutral way to discuss what is bad and good, or who is owed what (and also because their book was first published within the context of US-style individualism), "autonomy" became the first principle among equals. We saw above that both Macklin and Pinker want to replace the concept of human dignity with "autonomy." Autonomy has become the heart of our secularized culture of medicine and medical ethics.

Conclusion

Let's conclude this chapter by noting two things about what it means to equate our identity as human beings with the capacity to be autonomous. First, it comes from a particular understanding of the good that in many quarters is quite controversial. Second, in excluding human beings who don't have autonomous capacity, contemporary medicine and medical ethics have lost the concept of human dignity. And with it they have lost a sure basis for the fundamental and ultimate equality of all human beings. Recall a medical culture in which a Christian (or Jewish or Muslim) foundation could appeal to the fact that all human beings have dignity because of a shared nature that reflects the image and likeness of God. Claims about human equality do not follow from one's level of autonomy, self-awareness, rationality, productivity, or moral capacity, but from this shared nature. All humans are equal because we have a common nature which reflects the divine.

Given what you have just seen in this chapter, it should come as no surprise to hear that, for decades now, the understanding of the good at the heart of the theological claims mentioned above has been marginalized from medicine and medical ethics. Each of the next four chapters will focus on a particular category of human being who, as a result of this marginalization, has been excluded from the circle of protection afforded by human equality. As you read through these stories, histories, and arguments, I invite you to keep two questions in the back of your mind. First, when it comes to the question of who "we" are, where do you think our secularizing and irreligious trajectory is taking us? Where might we end up? Second, can you imagine a scenario in which Western culture (led at least in part by the institutions that got us into this mess in the first place) can recover a vision of the good within which we can also recover the concepts of human dignity and fundamental human equality?

Chapter Two

Jahi McMath and Brain Death

Jahi McMath's Catastrophic Brain Injury

It was the summer of 2014, and a thirteen-year-old girl named Jahi McMath had just reached puberty.[54] There would have been nothing at all remarkable about this development, except that, just a few months earlier, the State of California had declared that Jahi was dead. There was a death certificate and everything.

Jahi's family, however, refused to be bullied by California, or by the secularized medical community treating her, into accepting a vision of the good alien to their foundational beliefs. After routine surgery for sleep apnea, Jahi had received very poor medical care (more on this below) and an overlooked bleed led to full cardiac arrest. She survived this terrible ordeal but sustained such massive damage to her brain that she was largely unresponsive to stimuli and apparently in an unconscious state. She was able to use calories, water, and oxygen to keep the homeostasis of her body pretty much normal—as long as her medical team helped her get calories, water, and oxygen. Her body reached puberty and fought off infections; her hair and nails grew; her heart rate elevated and lowered when situations were stressful (surgery) or peaceful (when live music was played in her room). Young women in Jahi's situation who were pregnant at the time of their injury have even gestated their prenatal children on their way to becoming healthy newborn infants.[55]

Jahi's family was therefore on solid ground even on a biological basis in refusing to accept the judgment of Jahi's medical team and the State of California that, because her brain was (mostly) dead, their daughter was dead. They were also on solid ground philosophically, given what we just explored in the previous chapter. The State of California and her medical team judged that Jahi was dead not by medical facts, but according to answers to questions of ultimate concern based on a particular understanding of the good. Medical science and tests can be used to determine whether death has taken place, but *deciding what death is in the first place* can be determined only by asking theological questions. Nailah, Jahi's mother, and the rest of her family said that it's "not over until God says so" and filed a motion in court, arguing that their belief as Christians that Jahi's soul was still present as long as she had a heartbeat should be protected by religious freedom.[56]

Jahi's medical team was not receptive to her family's point of view. In fact, they were quite hostile to it. They outright dismissed as an "illusion" the idea that she was alive and declared it was an "absurd notion" that she might improve. David Durand, senior vice president and chief medical officer of the hospital where Jahi was admitted, was obviously annoyed by the family's persistence. "What is it that you don't understand?" Dr. Durand condescendingly asked them. And according to Jahi's mother, stepfather, grandmother, brother, and their lawyer, who took notes, Durand pounded his fist on the table, saying, "She's dead, dead, dead."

Maybe Durand really believed she was "dead, dead, dead," but another factor loomed for the hospital and their malpractice insurance company. If Jahi was dead, damages for malpractice related to her care after her routine surgery were capped at $250,000. If she were still alive, a jury could award an unlimited amount.[57] Not least because Blacks are so attuned to racial injustice in the delivery of health care, two hundred people, led by Black church leaders like Brian K. Woodson, Sr., the pastor of Bay Area Christian Connection, gathered in front of the hospital in a fierce protest of the injustice in Jahi's case. They marched and held signs that said "Justice for Jahi!" and "Doctors Can Be Wrong!" Many of Nailah's friends and neighbors participated—she lived in a close-knit community, very near her grandmother, who had moved to Oakland from Louisiana during the height of the civil rights movement. Refusing to bend to social injustice was in her family's blood.

Still, the hospital refused to honor their requests. The ethics committee was in one hundred percent agreement that further treatment of Jahi was inappropriate. They said, "No conceivable goal of medicine—preserving life, curing disease, restoring function, alleviating suffering—can be achieved by continuing to ventilate and artificially support a deceased patient." Those are big, confident, sweeping claims. Claims, frankly, that are not used to being challenged. But eventually, due to the indefatigable persistence of her family, the hospital agreed to release Jahi to the

Alameda County coroner, who would declare her dead, after which the family would become "wholly and exclusively responsible" for her.

Only two states—New Jersey and New York—allow the kind of religious freedom that Jahi's family was demanding, and they managed to get care for her at St. Peter's Hospital in New Brunswick, New Jersey. Even at this Catholic hospital, however, not everyone was interested in treating Jahi with human equality. Nailah spent nearly every waking hour at the hospital with her daughter and, after becoming friendly with some of the nurses, learned that the surgeon who performed a tracheotomy for her had been ostracized by his colleagues. "They were like, 'You operated on that dead girl?'"

That's pretty dismissive. But the reaction of many in secularized US medical ethics camps was even more so. At times it was downright hostile. Arthur Caplan, the go-to bioethicist for major US media, wrote, "Keeping her on a ventilator amounts to desecration of a body." And to *USA Today* he said, "You can't really feed a corpse. . . . She is going to start to decompose." Laurence McCullough, a medical ethicist at Cornell, couldn't believe St. Peter's even admitted Jahi. "What could they be thinking?" he also told *USA Today*. "There is a word for this: crazy." Another prominent bioethicist on end-of-life issues, Thaddeus Mason Pope, brought resource allocation into the picture. He told Rachel Aviv, a reporter for the *New Yorker*, that "every extra hour of nursing time that goes into one of these dead patients is an hour of nursing time that didn't go to somebody else."

One bioethicist who dissents from mainstream orthodoxy on brain death, Harvard's Robert Truog, has spent years trying to complexify the debate—but he has received similarly hostile pushback even for this effort. During an academic lecture in which he described living human beings like Jahi as having a "catastrophic brain injury," a transplant physician responded by saying, "You should be ashamed of yourself. What you are doing is immoral: to put doubts in the minds of people about a practice that is saving countless lives." Note again the concern for allocation of scarce medical resources (in this case, organs for transplant) as a central part of the objection. Happily, Truog was willing to take the fire and stood strong in resisting the consensus. He told Aviv, "I think that the bioethics community felt this need to support the traditional understanding of brain death, to the point that they were really treating the family with disdain, and I felt terrible about that."

New Jersey, not least due to effective lobbying from religious groups (especially Orthodox Jews) who insisted that their particular vision of the good be respected in medical practice, forbids insurance providers from denying medical coverage because of "personal religious beliefs regarding the application of neurological criteria for declaring death." This law allowed for Jahi to move out of the hospital and instead be treated in a New Jersey apartment (with home care). Alan Weisbard, the executive director of the bioethics commission that drafted the law, told Aviv, "I thought our position should be one of humility, rather than certainty." Significantly, he noted that "the people who have done the deep and conceptual thinking about brain death are people with high I.Q.s, who tremendously value their cognitive abilities—people who believe that the ability to think, to plan, and to act in the world are what make for meaningful lives. But there is a different tradition that looks much more to the body."

Precisely. But even with the move to the apartment, Nailah and her family couldn't avoid disdain from certain quarters of the community. One day, for instance, police showed up at their apartment after receiving a cruel anonymous tip that "there was a dead body in the house." After they saw that Jahi was getting air and food, and was obviously still a living human being, the cops quickly left the premises—but the damage had been done. What does it do to a family to face that kind of vitriol, especially when race was likely a motivating factor for the cruelty?

Indeed, throughout the process Nailah and her family sensed the racism. "No one was listening to us," she said. "And I can't prove it, but I really feel in my heart: if Jahi was a little white girl, I feel we would have gotten a little more help and attention." Nailah's mother, herself a nurse for thirty years, had told the nurses working with her daughter that Jahi's blood loss after surgery was not normal—and yet they couldn't get the medical team to move on the problem before it became catastrophic. These sorts of terrible events, major examples of racial injustice, are far too common in Black communities.

Brain Death, the End of Life, and Racial Justice

The history of medical racism in the United States is an utter embarrassment, a stain on the country, and a clear violation of the principle of fundamental human equality.[58] The terrible Tuskegee syphilis trials in which, among other things, none of the hundreds of men who participated were told of their diagnosis, in recent years have received significant coverage in the press and in schools. Less well known, however, is the fact that in medical schools both free and enslaved Blacks have been used without their consent to help teach anatomy. The graves of Blacks were robbed and bodies exhumed to use as educational cadavers. Blacks were used in radical surgical experiments.[59] For reasons that are not difficult to discern, many Black communities grew deeply distrustful of American medicine, and the distrust persists widely to this day.[60] This can be explained not simply on the basis of this shameful history, but also because actual racial prejudice (and not just structural racism, which is bad enough[61]) is still a significant problem in the delivery of US health care.[62]

In this context, the reaction of Jahi's family becomes even more understandable—even for those with a different view about brain death or human equality. And their family is hardly alone. When Pew asked whether "there are circumstances in which a patient should be allowed to die" or "medical staff should do everything possible to save a patient's life in all circumstances," a striking racial gap revealed itself.[63] Among whites, only 20 percent say everything possible should be done, but among Blacks, that number is 52 percent. Among Hispanics it is 59 percent. Distrust of the medical system which serves them at the end of life is so profound among Blacks that it even leads to skepticism of hospice—something that, for most white families, is close to an unquestioned good.[64]

As regular victims of what they perceive to be a racist medical system, racial minorities are quite attuned to the fact that certain populations are at risk "of becoming throwaway people."[65] Their dignity is inconvenient and thus they are far more likely to be forgotten or even discarded. It is more difficult for privileged white people (who dominate academic bioethics and medicine) to understand this perspective. Every so often we see an article by a physician encouraging us to die like physicians do—that is, without aggressive medical care at the end of life or when there is a profound disability.[66] But this misses the essential point that physicians are people of privilege who often have profoundly ableist and even consumerist attitudes about which lives matter. In my previous book, *Resisting Throwaway Culture*, I pointed out that physicians consistently rate the quality of life of their disabled patients worse than the patients themselves do.[67] The same has been found with disabled or sick adolescents and their families.[68] Disability bias in CPR providers leads them to consider some patients as "socially dead" and therefore unworthy of being saved.[69] Neonatologists often think that babies born with severe disabilities have fates worse than death.[70] And when confronted with the fact that patients generally prefer length of life to quality of life, physicians might feel "surprised" and admit, "We think we know what is best for a patient, but this is often wrong."[71]

The illusion of autonomy plays a large role here. Once a privileged person has an injury or disease and is disabused of the idea of being autonomous—especially in a consumerist culture like ours—such a person is much more likely than other populations to decide that life is no longer worth living. In Oregon loss of autonomy is the number one reason that people request assisted suicide, with over 90 percent citing it in 2014.[72] (Unsurprisingly, over 94 percent of those who requested suicide that year were white.) For privileged folks the huge role that autonomy plays in deciding whether or not a life is worth living is, well, not the same kind of problem for less privileged folks, whose life experience confirms that thinking we are autonomous beings is an illusion. As Jeff Bishop puts it, Western-style medicine as practiced today suffers from the myth of autonomy and the individual as sovereign—but hides the fact that, far from being sovereign subjects, we are very much at the mercy of social and philosophical power structures that shape our lives.[73]

Good Reasons to be Skeptical

It turns out that Jahi's family had more than enough cultural, historical, biological, and philosophical reasons to be skeptical of and ultimately reject the prevailing views in medicine and bioethics. In the experts' view Jahi was already dead, so they predicted (as we saw above) that her body would begin to decompose. Not only did this not happen (Jahi would go on to live four more years), but there is strong evidence that she responded to those addressing her. Nailah would regularly speak to Jahi, even telling her, "You have my permission to go. I don't want you here if you're suffering." But she then added, "If you can hear me and you want to live, move your right hand."[74] And, according to her mother, that right hand moved. Then she moved her other hand on command. Videos were released by the family that seemed to show Jahi moving her foot on request. Her mother even says she made a "thumbs up."

This evidence, in addition to her reaching puberty and getting her period, made the claim that Jahi was dead very strange indeed.[75] David Magnus, a Stanford University medical professor and director of Stanford's Center for Biomedical Ethics, said that if Jahi really did do the things seen on the video, "that would be a huge challenge, medically and scientifically. It means what people believe they know about brain death based on decades of experience and evidence would turn out to be false."[76] And it would be one thing if these views were coming only from Jahi's family, but as Aviv pointed out in her *New Yorker* piece, Jahi's doctors and nurses in New Jersey were converted to the position that she was still alive. Indeed, in Nailah's cell phone videos "several different nurses can be heard congratulating Jahi for gathering the strength and commitment to move a foot or a finger."[77] Aviv herself, who visited the apartment multiple times and spoke with dozens of people for her story, said she personally thought it was "unlikely" Jahi was not alive given "the weight of the evidence."

Jahi died of liver failure in 2018. This was, absurdly, four years after being declared dead by the State of California. An autopsy showed improvement in Jahi's brain function compared to her original MRIs.[78] It wasn't the first time a major mistake had been made along these lines: In 2008, after a major road accident, a young man named Zach was also thought to be brain dead. A transplant team was on the verge of taking his organs when, according to media reports, he "came back to life."[79] With not just hand movement, but hand squeezing. Then talking. Then walking. And these were certainly not isolated mistakes. One of the first major autopsy studies of patients who were considered brain dead found that 60 percent of the 226 patients did not have a fully dead brain.[80]

This fact has been emphasized by D. Alan Shewmon who, at the time of the drama surrounding Jahi, had just retired as the chief of the pediatric neurology department at Olive View-UCLA Medical Center.[81] Aviv noted that Shewmon, a long-time critic of the brain death criterion, had a profound conversion while listening to music as an undergraduate at Harvard. At the time he was an atheist who thought everything could be reduced to matter in motion, but his transcendent experience of the music provoked a complete change to his worldview. He converted to Catholicism, studied Aristotelian-Thomistic philosophy, and went on to spend a career thinking about the complex relationship between brain, mind, consciousness, and the living human body.

Over time, Shewmon grew uneasy with the standard use of brain death as indicating the death of the human person. Aviv describes him as discovering that its defenders could not offer a coherent defense of the standard without coming dangerously close to the Nazi concept of "Permission to Destroy Life Unworthy of Living." (It is revealing, especially for a central argument of this book, that the dramatic shifts in understanding of fundamental equality enacted by both the Nazi and Harvard programs were motivated in large measure by concerns over resource scarcity.[82]) Indeed, he noted they would usually end up admitting that these patients "were still living biological organisms" but had lost the capacities which made them equal to persons. In the late 90s Shewmon wrote an article titled "Recovery from 'Brain Death': A Neurologist's Apologia," in which he officially and publicly changed his mind. Despite the fact that "dissenters from the 'brain death' concept are typically dismissed condescendingly as simpletons, religious zealots or pro-life fanatics," he said, they were correct to reject the consensus. Shewmon was heavily involved in Jahi's case and served as an expert witness in several legal proceedings. Aviv notes that in one court declaration he said, "Given the evidence of intermittent responsiveness, we should be all the more willing to remain agnostic regarding her inner state of mind during periods of unresponsivity, rather than automatically equate it with unconsciousness."

The debate over Jahi's life shows the fragility of the supposed consensus over brain death. The concept is imprecise, leaky, and at times even incoherent. Unsurprisingly, it doesn't correspond to the way we almost always speak about life and death. A typical example can be found in this headline from an Associated Press story about a woman who, while pregnant, suffered the rupture of a cerebral aneurysm: "Brain-Dead Woman Gives Birth, Then Dies."[83] How did the dominant bioethics and medical community arrive at such a strange consensus? As we will see below, it was driven at first by allocation of scarce medical resources rather than by developing a coherent point of view on what death is and who "we" are.

Rejecting Human Equality at Harvard–and Beyond

Recall from the previous chapter the secularization of medicine and medical ethics in the late 1960s and early 1970s. Also around this time, the concept of vital organ transplant (e.g. heart, pancreas, liver) was coming into social consciousness as a viable option. As one might imagine, the great need for such organs far outstripped the supply. With the increasing use of ventilators to save the lives of people with catastrophic brain injuries, it became tempting to use the organs of these human beings to save the lives of other human beings on waiting lists to receive a life-saving vital organ. It is no accident, given the secularizing forces in play in medicine and medical ethics, that Harvard Medical School took the lead in addressing this problem by reconsidering the traditional definition of death passed on by a set of largely Christian religious institutions. Henry Beecher, the famed anesthesiologist and chairman of a Harvard committee that oversaw the ethics of experimentation on human beings, noted, "Every major hospital has patients stacked up waiting for suitable donors."[84] He was quite direct about the fact that a failure to change the definition of death meant that "the curable, the salvageable, can thus be sacrificed to the hopelessly damaged and unconscious who consume the time and space and money better devoted to those who could be helped."[85]

Beecher succeeded in petitioning his dean to establish what would become the famous 1968 *Ad Hoc* Committee of the Harvard Medical School to Examine the Definition of Brain Death. In several other contexts I've written about the formation of this committee and its decision, but I did so in perhaps the most detail when I was in conversation with the work of the deeply secular Princeton philosopher, Peter Singer. Though I disagree with Singer's ultimate conclusions about personhood and human equality, he is one of the few thinkers in his camp willing to call out what was actually going on within the committee and to speak precisely and directly about the huge implications of its decision. The discussion which follows is largely based on Singer's *Rethinking Life and Death* and my *Peter Singer and Christian Ethics.*[86]

The committee began its report by making this remarkable statement:

> Our primary purpose is to define irreversible coma as a new criterion for death. There are two reasons why there is a need for a definition: (1) Improvements in resuscitative and supportive measures have led to increased efforts to save those who are desperately injured. Sometimes these efforts have only a partial success so that the result is an individual whose heart continues to beat but whose brain is irreversibly damaged. The burden is great on patients who suffer permanent loss of intellect, on their families, on the hospitals, and on those in need of hospital beds already occupied by these comatose patients. (2) Obsolete criteria for the definition of death can lead to controversy in obtaining organs for transplantation.

Peter Singer's response presses in exactly the right place:

> The Harvard committee does not even attempt
> to argue that there is a need for a new definition
> of death because hospitals have a lot of patients
> in their wards who are really dead, but are being
> kept attached to respirators because the law
> does not recognize them as dead. Instead, with
> unusual frankness, the committee said that a
> new definition was needed because irreversibly
> comatose patients were a great burden, not
> only on themselves (why to be in an irreversible
> coma is a burden on the patient, the committee
> did not say), but also on their families, hospi-
> tals, and patients waiting for beds.

As bad as the official version of the committee's report was (and oh, was it bad), the draft version was even worse. The draft claimed that a "secondary" issue was that "there is a great need for tissues and organs of, among others, the patient whose cerebrum has been hopelessly destroyed, in order to restore those who are salvageable." When the dean of the medical school saw this draft he insisted that Beecher change it because "it suggests that you wish to define death in order to make viable organs more readily available to persons requiring transplants."

Singer calls out the implications of what this commit-tee actually did by noting that "the reasons given by the committee for redefining death—the great burden on the patients, their families, the hospitals and the community, as well as the waste of organs needed for transplantation—

apply in every respect to all those who are irreversibly comatose, not only those whose entire brain is dead." And I'd go even further than Singer, for there is no reason to stop at those who are irreversibly comatose. It was "patients stacked up waiting for donors" which motivated the change in determination of death in 1968, and that same motivation exists today. Recall the reaction by the transplant physician to Truog's insisting that what happened to Jahi and others should be called "catastrophic brain injury," and not death: "What you are doing is immoral: to put doubts in the minds of people about a practice that is saving countless lives." The issue raised was not whether Truog's views are correct; the issue was whether Truog's views will result in fewer lives saved. As Bryan Volck notes in his review of *The Anticipatory Corpse*, our current use of the brain death criterion is a perfect illustration of Bishop's thesis that medicine thinks of the dead body as normative. How else could we possibly get away with providing "a set of clinical signs and tests to distinguish life from death without persuasively establishing what the difference between life and death truly is"?[87]

The approach of the Harvard brain death committee was rightly described as *ad hoc*; the thing being aimed at was saving more lives by freeing up more medical resources. Tragically, to achieve their aim they gave up on the concept of fundamental human equality. The committee set the precedent that certain living, breathing, gestating, growing, puberty-reaching, infection-fighting, and homeostasis-maintaining human beings were not the moral or legal equal of other human beings. Only these kinds of human beings, and not others, could have their vital organs removed and put into someone else's body. Those who held power in medicine and then in politics quickly picked up this precedent. Twenty-seven states would soon rework their definition of death to reflect what the committee had proposed; today all fifty states accept it (with New Jersey and New York, as we saw, the only ones to offer a religious exemption).[88]

Human inequality won.

From Human Equality to Personal Equality

As should now be clear, the shift to accept brain death as death was not driven by genuine arguments over what counts as life and what counts as death. Instead, a decision was made to use some human beings as resources to make things better for others. But suppose a genuine argument is attempted, especially without acknowledging the religious principles that undergird human equality. As we saw in the introduction to this book, there has been a shift to determine the equality of human beings in terms of their value as "persons." A "person" is not merely a fellow living human being, but rather a being with certain traits or capacities—especially autonomy, rationality, and self-awareness. But even arguments based on traits like these are inconsistent in their application of principle. Even though Jahi appeared to exhibit something like self-awareness and rationality in responding to her family's requests, everyone in the secularized bioethics and medical community agreed that she was dead. It is true that she wasn't autonomous—but if that is the standard for being counted as equal, then many other vulnerable human beings are in deep trouble. In the conclusion of this book I will explore the logical consequences of applying the autonomy standard consistently, but (thank goodness) neither medicine nor the broader society seem ready to do so just yet.

Just beneath the surface of these discussions there lurk unspoken yet clear social factors related to the impulse to change our definition of death in order to maximize medical benefit. Indeed, in a post-Christian secularized culture I don't think that the implicit views of personhood, which seem to have won the day, can be separated from how we think about productivity, ability, and consumerism. Again, as Singer asks, what is the "burden" that the Harvard committee refers to if, as they claim, someone who is brain dead is totally unconscious? Very often the burden that we attribute to patients is not on the patient at all, but rather on us—as personal caregivers, certainly, but also as a community. If individuals like Jahi count as persons, then the mandate to care for them creates a substantial burden on health-care resources—and an even larger burden on our ability to get organs for transplants. Human beings who are not productive, who are disabled, and who are a net drain on resources are not considered the equals of those who are productive and able-bodied and who produce a net gain of resources.

The concept of fundamental human equality, by contrast, is a bulwark against utilitarian approaches that target the most vulnerable among us and discard them in the name of producing better consequences for others. Genuine human equality means that accidental traits like age, level of ability, reliance on others, level of self-awareness, rationality, or autonomy do not affect the fundamental value of human beings—which comes from their nature as human beings and nothing else. But this is precisely the concept that, in slouching toward brain death, our secularized medical culture has rejected.

It is important to acknowledge that the equality of human beings with a catastrophic brain injury does not mean (1) doing everything possible to keep them alive or (2) closing the door on their donating vital organs. Though it goes beyond the scope of this chapter to get into the arguments, those with such injuries—just like any other human being—should have the legal option (through advance directives or a surrogate decision-maker) to refuse or discontinue treatment and care that is extraordinary or burdensome.[89] Furthermore, like Truog, I believe we should explore how (again, through an advance directive or surrogate) someone with a catastrophic brain injury could still donate vital organs to save others.[90] In such cases, of course, it would be important to ensure that the equal dignity of those with a catastrophic brain injury (and other vulnerable populations) is not assaulted by other means. But as Truog told Rachel Aviv for her *New Yorker* article, even though "there is no scientific reason for believing them to be dead," facilitating organ donation in these cases is still "a morally virtuous thing to do and we ought to facilitate it. We are doing the right thing for the wrong reasons."

Conclusion

We need to be intellectually honest throughout the process of debates like this. Intellectual honesty means not only being forthright about what is motivating an argument, but also confronting directly how the reasoning of an argument on one issue can affect one's view of another related issue. It is significant that in the course of her thorough reporting Aviv noticed how the same mistakes being made for those thought to be brain dead were being made for those thought to be in a "vegetative" state.

This is the topic of our next chapter.

Chapter Three

Terri Schiavo and the Vegetative State

Terri's Profound Disability

Terri Schindler was a young faithful Catholic woman. She attended Mass weekly and encouraged those around her to do the same. Her brother, Bobby Schindler, had his ups and downs with the Church in his early adult life, but Terri persisted in encouraging him to attend Mass and live out their Catholic faith. In fact, when he confided in her that his girlfriend might be pregnant, she strongly reminded him that having an abortion was not an option. Later, when she met her future husband, Michael Schiavo, Terri insisted that they get the counseling required for her to marry a non-Catholic in the Church. After becoming Terri Schiavo, she grew frustrated that Michael wouldn't attend Mass with her as much as she'd have liked; nevertheless, she went each week like clockwork.[91]

Little did Terri or anyone else know that her religiosity would be at the heart of a tragic legal case that gripped the United States during the first few years of the twenty-first century. In 1990, at age twenty-six, Terri had a heart attack and, though she was revived, sustained significant brain damage and was deemed to be in a permanent vegetative state (PVS). Many medical professionals (especially those who practice neurology) now use different language to describe conditions like hers. But at the time physicians called it PVS—though it was not always clear what the term was meant to include. More will be said below about this history, but it is safe to say that someone deemed to be in a PVS had a very serious brain injury, with no hope for consciousness; however, it was not as dramatic as brain death. Medics of the day knew, for instance, that Terri was awake at times and asleep at others. That she breathed on her own. That she reacted to stimuli like light and sound.

Nevertheless, in 1998 her husband, Michael (who three years after Terri's injury had met and begun living with another woman), petitioned the State of Florida to remove her feeding tube and end her life. This was the beginning of a long legal battle—and bitter national debate—that would involve the Florida courts and legislature, Congress, the president, federal courts, the Vatican, hundreds of news segments, and thousands of often vitriolic personal attacks. Terri's parents insisted, based on their experts' testimony, that she was not in a PVS and that as a faithful Catholic she would not have accepted the idea that food and water could be denied to a human being who was not dying. Especially unacceptable would be aiming to end a disabled human being's life because it was considered not worth living. Terri ended up living until 2005, when her parents' legal options ran out. Michael Schiavo claimed that when Terri was twenty-two years old they had a conversation in which she said, "If I ever become a burden to anybody, don't let me live like that."[92] It is questionable whether this sounds like something a devout young Catholic would say. Indeed, a major part of the debate concerned just how religious Terri was and what a devout Catholic would have wanted in this situation. Ultimately, her husband's version of events won the day and her parents (who were willing to care for Terri at their own expense, if necessary) saw their forty-one-year-old daughter dehydrated and starved to death.

Religion was not only at the heart of the debate over what Terri would have wanted. It was at the heart of the national debate itself. Indeed, opposition to the position of Terri's parents was almost uniformly dismissive of its religious basis. The attack by Joshua Perry, a bioethicist at Vanderbilt University Medical Center, was a classic example of dismissive contempt for views coming from "Biblical BioPolitics."[93] Many millions of Catholics who cannot be lumped in with the "religious right" also rejected the removal of Terri's feeding tube (St. John Paul II, for instance, perhaps the most important voice for social justice of the late twentieth century, specifically intervened against removing food and water in cases like Terri's[94]). Nevertheless, Perry focused his fire on Evangelical figures like James Dobson of Focus on the Family and Tony Perkins of the Family Research Council. Whenever such figures expressed their desire to "save" Terri Schiavo, he put the word in quotes in an effort to dismiss it as "emotive" language. Also problematic for him were claims that Terri was a "disabled person" being "starved to death." According to Perry, this kind of language

> irresponsibly and destructively polarizes the political discourse about medical-legal issues along largely the same lines of pro-life/pro-choice abortion politics. . . . The slogans and phrases continually repeated by the Religious

Right when discussing Terri Schiavo and her legal case are now, unfortunately, poised to become permanent fixtures in the positive law of several states. Of particular concern is the threat to individual autonomy implicit in this post-*Schiavo* Biblical BioPolitics legislative agenda.

Let's underline what lies at the center of his view: concern about individual autonomy and abortion. We've already seen how secularized bioethics, with its unyielding focus on autonomy (and general unwillingness to engage certain transcendental goods and ultimate concerns), has undermined fundamental human equality, and in the next chapter we will explore further how abortion fits into the attack on fundamental human equality. But let us pause here to note that thinkers like Perry don't even bother to contest the position held by John Paul II, Tony Perkins, and James Dobson. It is enough for them simply to dismiss it as divisive, polarizing, and perhaps having implications for other issues they don't like. Perry, though he mocked the so-called religious right for referring to Terri as disabled, failed to address the views of actual disability organizations. If he had, he would have been forced to wrestle with the views of Not Dead Yet, which argued before a US House of Representatives subcommittee that "Terri Schiavo's case may be the tip of a very large and almost fully submerged iceberg."[95] He might also have had to acknowledge that "the majority of [people] in the disability community who support Not Dead Yet's positions are pro-choice," many "are gay or lesbian," and many "are atheist or agnostic."[96]

Maybe those who agree with Perry's views honestly believed that Terri, the person, had died and simply couldn't get their heads around claims that Terri was disabled, threatened with starvation and dehydration, and needed to be saved. This is similar to those who think that someone who is "brain dead" has indeed died; however, a human being in PVS clearly is still a living human being. It is human equality that is being rejected. Terri only needed help with feeding, not breathing, and interacted with her environment even more than Jahi did. Although she lived for fifteen years as a profoundly disabled human being, her husband chose a gravestone which claimed that Terri "departed this earth" on February 25, 1990 and was "at peace" March 31, 2005.[97] And he wasn't alone: the *New Yorker* referred to a proposal that Michael divorce Terri so that her parents would get "the rights to her body."[98] (This article, like so many others, also expressed deep concern about how a particular view of Terri's case could affect the abortion debate.) Academics used similar language: writing in the journal *Genome Biology*, Gregory Petsko highlighted the health-care workers who for many years had "nursed the body of Terri Schiavo."[99] On Court TV, Wesley Smith, one of the few bioethicists who has been fighting hard and publicly for fundamental human equality, put the matter of Terri's moral status directly to bioethicist Bill Allen:[100]

SMITH: Bill, do you think Terri is a person?

ALLEN: No, I do not. I think having awareness is an essential criterion for personhood. Even minimal awareness would support some criterion of personhood, but I don't think complete absence of awareness does.

Again, we will see below that a good percentage of people thought to be in PVS are, in fact, conscious and aware.

Given what we learned in the previous chapter, we should not be surprised that Allen's view can be advanced from a moral status to the allocation of scarce medical resources.[101] Here's more from the exchange cited above:

> SMITH: If Terri is not a person, should her organs be procured with consent?

> ALLEN: . . . Yes, I think there should be consent to harvest her organs, just as we allow people to say what they want done with their assets.

Allen was not alone in invoking the issue of scarce resources. The editors at the *Denver Post*, for instance, said that it is "one thing to see that money [is] used to keep Grandmother comfortable in her last years" but "another to spend it on keeping her unconsciously tied to tubes month after month—especially when the family wealth could have been assigned to the children's education."[102] And when the family's money runs out it's "the taxpayers, through Medicaid" who often finance the care—as they did for Terri Schiavo's care in Florida. "But should they?" the *Denver Post* editors ask. "There are arguments aplenty over the enormous sums being devoted to heroic end-of-life treatments, even when the ailing person is conscious. But the wisdom of using taxpayer dollars to keep people in irreversible comas or vegetative states is less debatable." Tyler Cowen, writing only three days before Terri's death, also expressed his concern that her care was being "financed by the state of Florida and Medicaid" and that it "costs $80,000 a year to keep her alive."[103] Ominously, especially given the concerns of the final chapter of this book, Cowen noted that the issues of such costs of care will become even more important as "Medicare grows as a percentage of the federal budget."[104]

Where We Are Today and How We Got Here

The debate over Terri's life, though it continues today (most often as a case study in college ethics courses), reached its crescendo about fifteen years ago. In the worlds of bioethics and technology this is an epoch. To understand the enormity of the changes since 2005, we need to go even further back to how injuries like the one Terri sustained had been understood previously. Arguably the most important expert on this topic is Joseph Fins, an attending physician and chief of medical ethics at New York Presbyterian Hospital and Weill Cornell Medical College. In addition to serving the Clinton administration as a policy advisor and as president of the American Society of Bioethics and Humanities, Fins's research and publications over the last two decades have led his colleagues to recognize him as one of the most eminent scholars of the ethics of brain injury and consciousness disorders.[105] I rely on his research and publications in the section that follows.

Interestingly (especially given the discussion of what one might call "secular religion" in chapter 1), Fins says, "The vegetative state has become something of a catechism in North American bioethics."[106] He provocatively claims that our current understanding of the vegetative state became "the moral predicate upon which the legal right to die was established and sustained." Add to this the mistaken view concerning the "perceived fixity" of the brain of someone deemed to be vegetative, and it is easy to see why certain interventions for such patients, even life-sustaining ones, have been almost uniformly resisted. Fins's work over the last several years has demonstrated, however, that this has been a profoundly misguided approach—one which led to "the marginalization of a highly vulnerable population."

Though he says it came as an inconvenient surprise for those "whose views were molded by the strong linkage of brain injury to the establishment of a right to die," many patients thought to be in a vegetative state can and do recover. This fact has been officially recognized by the relevant clinical organizations—like the American Academy of Neurology, the American College of Rehabilitation Medicine, and the National Institute on Disability, Independent Living and Rehabilitation Research—who, based on a thorough review of new clinical evidence, in September 2018 jointly published new practice guidelines on the care of patients with disorders of consciousness. Fins notes that the guidelines call for "improved standards of assessment and care, the use of emerging diagnostic and treatment modalities, as well as the prevention of medical complications that can confound diagnosis or adversely affect morbidity and mortality." For our purposes in this chapter, however, perhaps the most important change is that the permanent vegetative state has now been re-designated as the "chronic" vegetative state.

In 1994 a distinction was made between a persistent and a permanent vegetative state. In 2002 a "minimally conscious state" was distinguished from a vegetative state. In 2006 a study on a patient who was "clinically vegetative on examination" revealed that her brain activated its motor and spatial regions when she was asked to imagine herself playing tennis and then walking in her house. She was even able to answer correctly yes-or-no questions by imagining one or the other as her response. In his magisterial 2015 *Rights Come to Mind*, Fins tells the detailed stories of several patients thought to be vegetative but who ended up in a very different place.[107] One dramatic example is that of "Maggie," a patient with whom Fins interacted personally. After having a stroke during her senior year at Smith College, she was deemed to be in a vegetative state and would have remained mistakenly diagnosed if not for her neurologist, who discovered that she was trying to communicate by blinking. Studies of Maggie's brain later showed that the "perceived fixity" model must be abandoned. Her brain was rewiring itself. Fins points out that, although Maggie's case is particularly dramatic, it is just the latest acknowledgment of the capacity for PVS recovery.

Indeed, Fins's work reveals that cases like Maggie's are far from isolated. He cites replicated studies which show that an astonishing 40 percent of patients "thought to be vegetative" were "in fact in the minimally conscious state." The review of the clinical evidence leading to the new care guidelines found that 20 percent of patients thought to be permanently unconscious might regain consciousness. Given these facts, the move to describe a "vegetative state" as "chronic" instead of "permanent" was a long time coming. Fins rightly notes that, if the United States had been in a normal news cycle at the time (that is, not one dominated by presidential politics), the dramatic report from these clinical organizations would have made headlines—and would have rocked the world of bioethics.[108]

Why does Fins use such dramatic language? Because in his view the perceived fixity of the vegetative state was central to the iconic right-to-die cases, including that of Terri Schiavo. The "key question," he insists, "is whether acknowledging that the vegetative state is not what we thought it was undermines the hard-won right to die." He says that it was "reassuring," historically, to rely on the very clinical judgments which have now been discarded as mistaken. But now he asks, could what we've learned "undermine one of the central accomplishments of early bioethics—namely, advancement of patients' and families' dominion over choices about how they live and die"? Harkening back to abortion (which, tellingly, comes up again and again in these debates), Fins compares the abandoned consensus on the fixed nature of the vegetative state to a similarly abandoned consensus on fetal viability. The latter was central to the trimester framework employed in *Roe v. Wade*, but discrediting it eroded at least some arguments for abortion rights. Could something similar happen to "the hard-won right to die"? Could this even lead to an "assault on self-determination" itself?

Short answer: not necessarily. Both Fins and I agree that, even in circumstances where there is consciousness, there will be times that life-sustaining treatment can and even should be withdrawn (especially when the patient can communicate wishes for no extraordinary treatment). But the way Fins asks the questions above is quite revealing about what is at stake here. We will return to this when we consider how these patients may be treated in the future. But let us finish this section by giving Fins the last word on what the new findings might mean for how we view Terri's case:

> Recoveries out of the formerly "permanent" vegetative state will prompt us to revisit the debate over Terri Schiavo, a case that divided her family and the nation. If some patients whose consciousness was thought to be irretrievably lost can return from that great unknowing beyond, is it ever proper to withhold or withdraw care? If we hang on long enough, won't some of these people recover? Without the futility of the permanent vegetative state, of permanent unconsciousness, are we obliged to promote a "culture of life"?

A Call for Basic Civil Rights

Fins resists the idea that we might be obligated to promote a culture of life, but he is eager to defend what he calls the basic civil rights of these vulnerable populations. He begins by calling out the clinical response of "prognostic pessimism" and "therapeutic nihilism" to most patients who may be chronically vegetative or minimally conscious. Despite "stunning evidence to the contrary"—much of it just explored above—the dominant clinical view is that nothing can be done beyond palliative care. Some of this, Fins says, borders on the ideological—with physicians "bringing their own biases forward" via directive counseling designed to engineer the outcomes they want.[109]

If a family does manage to fend off attempts to push them toward removing life-sustaining treatment, care for their injured family member is likely to be at best second-rate. Fins laments that current clinical practice results in large numbers of these patients lingering in long-term care facilities without access to adequate medical management or rehabilitation. The explanation for this neglect comes back to an ideology based on (as I point out throughout this book) a certain perspective of the good. In this case, it is a certain perspective on personhood. Fins cannot hide his frustration when he describes how Maggie "had been depersonalized" by the medical team. She had been "turned into someone—or something—who seemingly had no interests and in whom others would have no interest." And this, he is at pains to point out, is also not an isolated case, because

> patients with disorders of consciousness have been prone to depersonalizations, almost relegated to the status of nonpersons and hence deprived of the respect that has been linked to personhood. It is an irony and a tragic one, because the very principle articulated to guarantee respect for the most vulnerable of persons

> [respect for persons under the Belmont Report]
> has been unable to protect individuals most in
> need of it.

While the principle of respect for persons may be used to defend certain vulnerable human beings, in many cases a particular vision of personhood is invoked specifically to exclude and marginalize other vulnerable human beings. It is good that Fins sees what is happening here, but for those who recognize how personhood is used to exclude, there is nothing "ironic" at all about it. This is precisely how the ideological game has been played so that those with power can achieve the outcome they desire—an outcome which at times includes discarding human beings whose dignity they find inconvenient.

We have already seen in some detail how this game is closely connected to a shift away from an explicitly religious vision of the good which supports the fundamental equality of every single human being, and toward a secularized vision which speaks of personal equality on the basis of actualized traits like autonomy. Especially in light of what we've seen thus far in this chapter, it is worth thinking about how religious families are treated when they want standard treatment and therapy for an injured family member. Though Fins is spot-on and even courageous in challenging the powers and structures that perpetuate these injustices, the word "secular" does not appear in *Rights Come to Mind*. This is strange, not just because of the centrality of religion in the debates over vegetative state, but also because the case studies that Fins himself uses are often permeated with religious concerns. He quotes the mother of a brain-injured woman named Sharon, for instance, saying that the family immediately got "in touch with our priest." They were Catholic and wanted to be sure that "any crucial decisions" were "the right ones in terms of our conscience, and our faith, and what was best for Sharon."

Unfortunately, given the dominant ideology within the medical community, those families whose religious faith leads them to care for their brain-injured relative as the equal of any other human being will run into a system that resists anything resembling religious motives. Fins speaks of "indifference, a lack of professionalism, poor care, and even negligence" of these brain-injured populations. One of the people he interviewed for *Rights Come to Mind* even mentioned that their nursing home had a floor where the staff "just put everybody who had no opportunity, or no prospect of ever being very alive. Alzheimer's patients, people who were in PVS. So they had this horrible second floor. If you went up there it was filthy, the staff was bad." (Keep the image of this floor in mind for our discussion in chapter 6.)

Such evidence suggests that Fins may not fully appreciate the relationship between religion and secularization in all of this. For those who have been trained in medicine and/or medical ethics during the past two generations, a secularized culture is simply the water in which virtually everyone is swimming. ("What is water?" said the fish.) Nevertheless, he understands that something is fundamentally wrong and needs to change. He is courageously imploring his colleagues in medicine not to abandon or segregate a whole set of people. Well aware of the historical undertones of the phrase, he insists that the current situation is yet another failure of the idea that we can have "separate but equal" institutions. Basic civil rights for the populations on which this chapter focuses mean that patients and their families should be "maximally integrated into the community." Failure to identify those who are conscious and place them in proper rehabilitative settings, with proper pain medication and management, is a "fundamental miscarriage of justice and civil rights." Brain-injured patients "make a justice claim" on medicine that they be given an equal chance to benefit from new technologies which could restore or augment their abilities. Fundamental human equality requires nothing less. Just as we have a social responsibility to educate children with developing brains, says Fins, we have a social responsibility to rehabilitate and educate older people with injured brains capable of further development.

But as we saw at the end of the section on Terri Schiavo, many worry about what such equal treatment would cost. Fins cites a paper from the *Journal of the American Academy of Neurology* which even recommends that clinicians emphasize to the family just how expensive care of their brain-injured family member will be—even if it is paid for by private or public insurance. Fins rejects any objections that would keep patient and family preferences from being fully heard, but in the short term there is little that can be done if insurance companies refuse to get on board. Companies often refuse access to rehabilitation for those who are deemed to be in a vegetative state, and make little or no attempt to see if the patients could be or are minimally conscious. It is not difficult to identify the major reason: cost. Fins tells the story of Andrea, who advocated at every turn for her husband Wayne (who was in a minimally conscious state). But her appeal of their insurance company's denial resulted in her paying massive out-of-pocket expenses for his medical care: $400/month for drugs and more than $600/day for rehab. At the time of the interview with Fins, she had spent $170,000 of their own money for his care.

These are sobering numbers and Fins, like all of us should be, is realistic about what can be done when resources are limited. But this vulnerable population shouldn't expect special or disproportionate treatment, he says; rather they should receive equal treatment combined with study and use of cost/benefit analysis. He offers what he calls a "modest policy agenda" that details what we owe these populations. But he is also "under no illusions that it will be readily achieved." There are too many cultural and structural headwinds. The depersonalization that dominates clinical reactions and practices has even prevented this obviously disabled population from receiving the protections and benefits of the Americans with Disabilities Act. Fins's deeply admirable crusade is to take action, along the same lines as other civil rights movements, to recognize the fundamental equality of this vulnerable and voiceless population.

What Does the Future Hold?

Even the originator of this new civil rights struggle admits that in the short term things aren't likely to change. But what about the medium or longer term? Will those who practice secularized medicine and bioethics heed Fins's call for activism? Will we admit and even emphasize the fundamental equality of these brain-injured populations and act accordingly? The current secularized trajectory invites skepticism. There are at least three prevailing reasons in secularized medicine and bioethics for continuing, as Fins puts it, to "look away" from what we've learned and "hold tight to therapeutic nihilism."[110] First, the commitment of health-care resources is just too large. Second, for those who agree with it, the "hard-won" right to die may be at stake. Third, rethinking the Terri Schiavo case—and more broadly the moral status of all disabled human beings in a chronic vegetative state—may risk setting in motion a return to an ethic of human equality that calls into question the settled doctrine of brain death and the marginalization of prenatal human beings. Let us consider each of these reasons.

First, as we saw with brain death, the tail actually was wagging the dog when it came to the moral status of brain-dead human beings. They weren't considered dead until their being alive posed a problem for those who wanted access to their body components for organ donation. We saw above that at least one prominent bioethicist was willing to say on television that Terri Schiavo was a non-person and therefore could have her vital organs taken from her. This view is broadly shared within the medical community: two-thirds of physicians would support taking vital organs from a patient in a (so-called) vegetative state.[111] And for more than two decades bioethicists have been making strong arguments for taking vital organs from patients in this situation.[112] Maryland's state legislature has moved to have non-vital organs removed from vegetative patients without their consent, and has even discussed removing vital organs.[113] In addition to organ donation, the daunting costs of treating and attempting to rehabilitate the severely brain-injured loom large here as well. Remember Beecher's ominous point that a failure to change the definition of death meant that "the curable, the salvageable, can thus be sacrificed to the hopelessly damaged and unconscious who consume the time and space and money better devoted to those who could be helped."[114] Respecting fundamental human equality, from this perspective, just consumes resources that could be put to better use elsewhere.

Second, recall how closely Fins connected the outdated understanding of vegetative state to the development of a central accomplishment of secularized bioethics and medicine:

- The fixity of vegetative state was the "moral predicate" on which the right to die was established.

- The "iconic" right-to-die cases rely on the now-debunked understanding of vegetative state.

- The "key question" is whether acknowledging that the old notion of vegetative state is mistaken "undermines the hard-won right to die."

- What we've learned about vegetative state may "undermine one of the central accomplishments of early bioethics" that gave patients and families free choice about dying.

Those who advance secularized bioethics are, generally speaking, not as open-minded as Fins and therefore unlikely to revisit their views and practices in these areas—especially because the moral and legal accomplishments in which they take the most pride rely explicitly on the doctrines from which Fins dissents. At least without a shift away from the secularizing and even irreligious trends over the last five decades and toward an explicit welcoming of a religious focus on fundamental human equality, it is difficult to imagine that significant numbers of ethicists and clinicians will reconsider something which would in turn force them to reconsider the right to die.

Third and finally, the connections between vegetative state and brain death are obvious: if we were wrong about the moral status of those with brain death, then *boy were we wrong* about those in a chronic vegetative state. But we must also notice how often abortion is invoked in these arguments. Acknowledging that human beings like Terri have fundamental equality with all other human beings simply because of their common humanity would have clear implications for acknowledging the fundamental humanity of prenatal human children—and on the same basis. And to be fair, this is why a good number of anti-abortion pro-lifers also care so deeply about the debates over severely brain-injured populations. The toxicity of abortion politics infects all the issues we will look at in this book. But with respect to the topic of this chapter, the ferocity with which secularized bioethicists and clinicians hold onto abortion rights is likely to keep the debate over the moral status of disabled humans in a chronic vegetative state largely right where it is.

Conclusion

This chapter has illustrated a second important factor that has undermined fundamental human equality: the marginalization of disabled patients in a vegetative state. It is no surprise that what is happening to this population has significant overlap with what is happening to brain-dead human beings. It is part of a natural and logical progression, especially when our cultural debates over health care center upon issues of resource allocation. We must resist these trends toward wrongful discrimination against the disabled (ableism) and toward an idolatrous consumerism by acknowledging a paradigm in which all human beings, no matter which abilities (autonomy, consciousness, communication, and so on) they possess or do not possess, are fundamentally equal simply because they share in the dignity stemming from a common nature that bears the image and likeness of God.

Fins would at least appear to disagree with this, my central thesis in this book. After all, he does not seem interested in fundamental human equality, but rather in whether a patient is or could be conscious. Not all living human beings are equal, in his view, but only certain specified human beings who count as persons. For human beings who are "vegetative" for an extended period of time, such that we think they will never be conscious again, their lack of potential means that they do not share in our fundamental equality. It is admirable that Fins is willing to push his view of personhood in ways which challenge the bioethics establishment, especially because accepting that the mere potential for consciousness grants personhood has deep implications for the moral status of prenatal and neonatal human beings. (More to come on this in the next chapter.) But it does leave out those human beings who lack such potential, at least as Fins understands the term.[115]

Many pro-lifers find the term "vegetative" offensive because it assaults the equal dignity of human beings with a shared nature. It is deeply mistaken to consider a brain-damaged human being to be "vegetative" simply because her functional capacities seem to resemble those of non-sentient living organisms. Indeed, recognizing that someone in a vegetative state *had an injury in the first place* demonstrates that we understand her nature to be quite different from that of a vegetable. Something accidental about her—her injury—is currently frustrating her ability to express fully her nature, the kind of thing that she is. When Maggie's brain rewired itself and she regained consciousness and the ability to communicate, she didn't go from being a vegetable to being a human being (or, to use Aristotle's categories, from having a vegetative soul to having an animal or rational soul[116]). No, throughout the process of recovering consciousness she had the same nature and the same moral status, and was the same kind of thing as she always had been.

Two decades ago almost everyone thought that vegetative states were fixed and permanent. But with the therapies Fins mentions, along with technologies like vagus nerve stimulation,[117] we now know that about 20 percent of diagnosed patients can be coaxed into varying levels of conscious states. But it will not do to say, "Well, we were wrong about 20 percent who we now acknowledge should have the moral and legal equality of persons. But the other 80 percent? They are 'vegetative' and don't have fundamental equality with the rest of us." What will happen when, with new technologies, we find that another chunk of those 80 percent can also regain consciousness? Or that, because we don't fully understand what consciousness is (some important thinkers and researchers are now arguing that it is a product of the human body, holistically considered, not just the brain[118]), we discover that consciousness does not depend entirely on having a working brain? We can't keep insisting that we were wrong about the cases where we discover consciousness where none existed before, but we continue to be right about the living human beings in which we have as yet discovered no such potential. Instead, we should acknowledge that moral status—and fundamental human equality—is based on the nature of an individual, based on the *kind of thing* they are. And in *our* case, the kind of thing is a human animal.

Fins comes close to saying something like this. When engaging bioethicist William J. Winslade, who maintains that a person must have "the ability to communicate and interact with other people," Fins offers an interesting response:

> While I do not agree that the vegetative state equates with the forfeiture of our humanity, as we humans live on in the memories of others and in the acts of goodness we performed while we were able, I do agree that we lose the ability to *act* [original emphasis] as persons when we lose our ability to communicate with others.[119]

87

I don't agree that a human being continues to live via the memories of others or via their own good deeds. People who have been dead for centuries or even millennia can "live" in this way too—but presumably Fins wasn't comparing a living disabled human in a vegetative state to humans who lived three thousand years ago. Nevertheless, he is very close here to making the distinction between the nature of a being (in her humanity) and "the ability to act" on or express that nature. This distinction is fundamental to the argument of this book. Does the fact that Fins is very close to making it mean his colleagues in bioethics and medicine could be too? One can hope.

This is pure speculation, but given how often he references and emphasizes the hard-won bioethics battles of the past, I wonder whether he (and his colleagues) hesitate to go "all the way" on the equality of vegetative patients because they worry that rethinking the moral status of human beings in a vegetative state will require us to rethink the moral status of prenatal human beings. It is to this topic we now turn.

Chapter Four

The "Roe Baby" and Abortion

In the lead-up to the marginalization of human beings with catastrophic brain injuries, we saw that the tail had been wagging the dog. The fundamental equality of these human beings got in the way of what was considered a more significant concern: getting vital organs to save the lives of other human beings. Similarly, this chapter will show that the fundamental human equality of prenatal human beings got in the way of more than one concern considered more significant: protection of physicians from prosecution, respecting the moral authority of physicians, controlling the births of human beings generally, controlling the births of disabled people in particular, and the economic (and social) status of women in relation to men. These issues, as with brain death, generated a new moral and legal vision focused on personhood—one that continued the trend of rejecting fundamental human equality.

But they do not and cannot replace the truth of fundamental human equality. The baby who started it all was very much a baby.

The Fate of the "Roe Baby"

Many have at least heard of the 1973 Supreme Court decision *Roe v. Wade*, in which seven unelected men declared that women have a legal right to have an abortion at any stage of pregnancy in the United States. Few, however, are aware that the child whose existence set in motion the series of events leading to that case was actually born and put into the arms of her mother, Norma McCorvey (the "Jane Roe" from *Roe v. Wade*), who later called her the "Roe baby." Upon finding out that she was pregnant for a third time, Norma had searched a good chunk of Texas to find someone who would do an illegal abortion. But she came up empty and was left with adoption as her only option for cutting the child out of her life. Toward that end, right after birth the baby was to be whisked away for transfer to adoptive parents.

But in her 1994 autobiography *I Am Roe* the then-prochoice activist detailed the dramatic events that unfolded:[120]

> Another few hours. Another nurse. This one had a bundled-up baby in her arms.
>
> "Feeding time!" she said.
>
> "What?"
>
> "Feeding time!" she said, again. Then she handed me the baby.
>
> I can't tell you all the horrible feelings that went through me at that moment. It was like getting a glimpse of hell—all my shame and fear and guilt and love and sadness all rolled up into a ball and placed in front of me.
>
> Was this my baby? Why were they giving it to me? Should I look at it or not look at it?

I was too full of pain to say anything. Through the blanket, I could feel the baby moving. Breathing.

There was a flap of cloth over its face. My entire body, my entire soul cried out to me to turn the flap down, to look at the baby's face. But my mind told me that it would be the worst thing I could ever do.

My mind won. My heart lost. I never touched the flap. I felt sick to my stomach. I started crying, loudly, in pure despair.

The nurse must have seen the expression on my face, because she quickly realized that she'd done something awful and ran out of the room. I was left alone with the baby, paralyzed, for another minute or two.

The nurse rushed back in, this time with two orderlies. She pulled the baby out of my arms and handed it to an orderly, who left. Then the baby was gone forever.

Her description of this encounter is truly powerful. The first time I read it, I felt my stomach almost torn in two. Especially when I thought about what the events surrounding this child would mean for other very young children across the United States (and their mothers) for decades to come.

How did Norma end up in a place so full of profound pain? Throughout her childhood she was abused (sexually and otherwise) multiple times by multiple people—including a marriage to an abusive husband when she was just sixteen. After that marriage ended, she got pregnant by a different man. She became severely addicted to alcohol and other drugs. The baby was placed for adoption. In Texas in the 1960s she identified as a lesbian and dated women. She got pregnant again and this second baby was also placed for adoption.

Nearly everyone in Norma's life failed her, many used her, and several even assaulted her. I cannot imagine the despair and helplessness her life's trajectory had reached when in 1969, at the age of twenty-one, she became pregnant for a third time, this time with her "Roe baby." On some level she felt tremendous regret over being disconnected from her two previous children, and Norma decided that she could not go through the process of adoption again. Keeping the child didn't seem like an option because she had no resources, so she pursued every possible avenue to obtain an illegal abortion—even trying to make her situation seem more sympathetic by claiming (falsely) that her pregnancy was due to rape.

She was totally and utterly consumed with not being pregnant. She asked her doctor to do an illegal abortion, but he refused and instead put her in touch with an adoption agency. Again, consumed with an overwhelming urge to escape her situation, Norma even asked the adoption agency to help her get an abortion. The agency informally referred her to two ambitious young lawyers who were trying to get Texas's abortion restrictions thrown out in court. (By this time, states like New York and California had already legalized abortion—the latter state's law being signed by Republican governor Ronald Reagan.) "Linda and Sarah," as Norma referred to them, didn't seem to care about her personal situation as much as they cared about using it to win their case. Indeed, they let Norma believe that if their lawsuit succeeded she could get the abortion she was seeking. After all, Norma reasoned, she had been to court before and things went pretty quick.

Linda and Sarah won their case. Judges in Texas ruled that abortion was legal, and Norma asked her lawyers if that meant she could now get an abortion. Her lawyers, of course, knew that an appeal was coming but brought that up only at this later date. Norma asked how long it would take. They responded, "A while. But, Norma, why does it matter? An abortion has to be performed in the first twenty-four weeks of pregnancy and it is clearly too late for you now." Norma described her world stopping with this "horrible, tragic, but also life-changing" realization. She noted astutely, however, that sometimes a terrible moment like that can open the door to truth pouring into one's life. At that moment she realized that, going forward, the legal case was not for the good of Norma McCorvey. She was also confronted with the fact that this, her "third child, the Roe baby" was "still moving inside" her and, despite the fact that she had no way of supporting the child, was going to be born. Upon realizing that they didn't have her interests in mind, Norma stormed out of Sarah and Linda's office, once again filled with white-hot anger and overwhelming despair.

Though Norma came to terms with the human life inside of her, the Supreme Court case bearing the name

Jane Roe did not. Indeed, even though in her book—from which the story relayed above comes—she says that she supports abortion rights completely, Norma was keen to point out that she didn't have much to do with the actual fight in *Roe v. Wade*. Her lawyers worried that the case would be thrown out if Norma was too far along in her pregnancy and thus unavailable for an abortion. So, without telling her, they added a class action lawsuit on behalf of women in general who were in her situation. Their argument was that abortion couldn't be murder because, at least as Norma explains it, "nobody knew if, or more important, when a fetus was considered a person under the law." She also noted that the deciding judges in *Roe* were concerned with whether a fetus had "the capability of a meaningful life." This argument won the day (as we will see in more detail below), but Norma explained that she heard about the 1973 *Roe* decision on the news, like everyone else did. In fact, she said she didn't hear from Sarah or Linda again until 1984. Amid the pitched battle to keep *Roe* in place against fierce public resistance (a battle that continues to this day), they asked her to go public as "Jane Roe" as part of their defense strategy.

The "real" Norma McCorvey, who later in life was celebrated as a pro-life activist, remains elusive. A 2020 *Fx* documentary purports that in a "deathbed confession" Norma claimed to have supported the pro-life movement because she was paid to.[121] But it is true that after she wrote *I Am Roe*, she was baptized as a Christian and at least publicly identified as pro-life. In a second biography, *Won by Love*, she says "I think I have always been pro-life. . . . I just didn't know it." Although she seems to have taken various positions in the abortion debate, it is clear that Norma McCorvey—whether seen as pro-choice or pro-life—had almost nothing to do with the core issues of the Supreme Court case that bears her pseudonym. The primary focus of *Roe v. Wade* was protecting professionals.

The Supreme Court's Focus: Protecting Physicians

No less an authority than Justice Ruth Bader Ginsburg herself lamented that the central concern of the argument in the *Roe v. Wade* decision was not the rights of women.[122] The long-time pro-choice *New York Times* beat reporter covering the Supreme Court, Linda Greenhouse, used even stronger language and added important details that relate to a major theme of this book:

> To read the actual opinion, as almost no one ever does, is to understand that the seven middle-aged to elderly men in the majority certainly didn't think they were making a statement about women's rights: women and their voices are nearly absent from the opinion. It's a case about the rights of doctors—fellow professionals, after all—who faced criminal prosecution in states across the country for acting in what they considered to be the best interests of their patients.[123]

Noah Feldman, professor of constitutional law at Harvard University, says that his students are also deeply surprised by what they find in the actual argument of *Roe*. "To a remarkable degree," notes Feldman, "the opinion is about doctors."[124] He points out that this is established in the second paragraph of the opinion, written by Justice Harry Blackmun, who was setting out his view that when it comes to abortion "medical expertise should make a difference to our legal thinking."

Indeed, Feldman points out that in Blackmun's opinion, he is concerned not only with Jane Roe, but with another party to the case: James Hubert Hallford, described as "a licensed physician" who "had been arrested previously for violations of the Texas abortion statutes," and who was facing further legal action. Blackmun's opinion invests with substantial authority the history of the medical community's opinion on abortion, as well as recent shifts in the views of groups like the American Medical Association. Even when discussing the right to privacy, which provides the foundation for the opinion, Blackmun is clear that it applies to a woman in consultation with her responsible physician. Later, when discussing viability, Blackmun drops the woman out of the scenario altogether: "The attending physician, in consultation with his patient, is free to determine, without regulation by the State, that, in his medical judgment, the patient's pregnancy should be terminated." Feldman notes rather dramatically that Roe "transfers responsibility for the woman's decision from the state to the physician—with the woman's control over her own body almost an afterthought by the end of the opinion."

Significantly, Blackmun's opinion mentions the word "physician" forty-eight times but the word "woman" only forty-four times.[125] After all, during his decade as general counsel for the famed Mayo Clinic in Rochester,

Minnesota, Blackmun developed a reverence for physicians. Those years, as Greenhouse reports in her biography of the Supreme Court justice, were the "happiest of his professional life."[126] The summer before he delivered the opinion in *Roe*, Blackmun spent his time poring through books in the Mayo Clinic's library on the history of physicians and abortion—the presumption being, again, that what physicians thought and did was authoritative simply because they were physicians. David Garrow reported that evidence of Blackmun's central concern for physicians goes back to his lament during a conference among the justices that the Texas law did "not go far enough to protect doctors."[127]

Blackmun and others interested in making sure physicians were not prosecuted for illegal abortions had good reasons to be concerned. As Clarke Forsythe points out, in the nineteenth and twentieth centuries US law considered women the second victims of abortion, focusing instead on prosecuting those who actually performed the act.[128] Indeed, physicians facing prosecution for illegal abortions would sometimes argue in their defense that the women were accomplices. If no one could corroborate the woman's testimony to the contrary, then her claims would be dismissed and likely the case along with it. Even years after *Roe* was decided, the goal of protecting physicians from liability remained a central concern.[129] Physicians, already in a professional class with profound advantages when it comes to avoiding legal consequences for their actions, are particularly good at avoiding criminal liability. This point was made quite powerfully by Sheri Fink in her book *Five Days at Memorial*.[130] She suggested that the medical community rallied in defense of Dr. Anna Pou, who was facing potential prosecution for illegally euthanizing patients in the aftermath of Hurricane Katrina, at least in part because if this Rubicon were crossed all of them could be at risk for criminal accountability to the law.

Strong evidence of Blackmun's concern about physicians runs through the text of *Roe*. But it couldn't be more clear than when, in the opening lines of the decision, he describes the right to abortion in the first trimester: "The abortion decision and its effectuation must be left to the medical judgment of the pregnant woman's attending physician." And in the companion case decided at the same time, *Doe v. Bolton*, Justice Blackmun defended a physician's judgment in shockingly broad ways. A woman could procure an abortion, even into the third trimester, if her "attending physician" deemed that her pregnancy might affect her physical, emotional, or psychological health and it was, in the physician's judgment, "relevant to the wellbeing of the patient." Above all, unsurprisingly, Blackmun was concerned to give the physician "the room he needs to make his best medical judgment."[131]

Perhaps Blackmun thought that giving physicians such power and latitude would benefit mothers as well, but Greenhouse—as her quote above implies—is deeply skeptical about this possibility. Indeed, it seems to her that Blackmun spent much of his career annoyed by the activism of feminists, including that of Ruth Bader Ginsburg during her time as general counsel for the ACLU Women's Rights Project.[132] Greenhouse is keen to point out that the handful of feminist activists attempting to drive the abortion debate toward *Roe* employed a very different ideology from the one offered in *Roe*, and that the major institutions pushing for abortion rights were not feminist in their orientation.[133] At the forefront were those concerned with "population growth" (spurred on by Paul Ehrlich's embarrassingly inaccurate predictions in *The Population Bomb*[134]) and, yes, activist physicians protecting their territory. Forsythe notes that as early as 1954, Dr. Alan Guttmacher, who served as president of both Planned Parenthood and the American Eugenics Society, engaged in influential activism for abortion rights.[135] Dr. Bernard Nathanson (though he would go on to have a Norma McCorvey-like conversion and join the pro-life movement[136]) was at the forefront of the debate as co-founder of the National Association for the Repeal of Abortion Laws (NARAL) in 1969. Forsythe also draws attention to the influence of the American Medical Association's formally changing their view on abortion during their summer meetings of July 1970. Their revised policy statement played a significant role in Blackmun's decision.

Simply put: the authority of medicine and of physicians, along with a concern to protect them from prosecution, cannot be overstated as motivating factors behind the *Roe v. Wade* decision and the marginalization of prenatal human beings.

Population Reduction, Eugenics, and Resource Concerns

The two previous chapters showed how concerns about resources played a significant role in undermining fundamental equality for vulnerable human beings. A good example of this in the context of the abortion debate is the unholy connection between the twin goals of population reduction and eugenics, especially as pursued by the privileged classes of the day. Forsythe notes that, by the late 1960s, claims about a "population crisis" had become a central and urgent part of the US national conversation. John D. Rockefeller III, an aggressive proponent of using abortion as a means of population control, led a (Republican) presidential commission geared toward doing precisely that. The judge who struck down Connecticut's abortion law in April of 1972 repeatedly cited both the Rockefeller commission and Ehrlich's *The Population Bomb* in his opinion. Forsythe also quotes this abstract of a widely influential article published by Dr. Richard A. Schwartz in August 1972:

> The yearly number of unwanted children born in the United States is 800,000, or 20 percent of all births. Forty percent of all births in poor families are unwanted. Because of the limitations of contraception, the most feasible way of decreasing the incidence of unwanted births is legalization of abortion. If all unwanted births could be prevented, this would lower the birth rate in the United States by more than 50 percent, substantially lower the incidence of poverty, and lead to a decrease in the number of inadequately reared children potentially destined to become criminals, psychotics, drug addicts, and alcoholics.

Forsythe also shows that an informal "eugenics and population control network" funded much of the abortion advocacy that led to *Roe*.

Planned Parenthood initially took pains to show that they were not advocating for abortion, which they described in their own 1952 literature as killing "the life of a baby after it has begun."[137] This was to change, however, largely because of the intervention of a male abortion-rights-activist physician: Dr. Guttmacher. As head of Planned Parenthood's medical committee, Guttmacher's abortion activism redirected the organization to consider abortion an integral part of medical care. At the heart of his arguments was a concern about so-called overpopulation. In a 1968 interview for WLBC-TV, he made it clear that his concern was about resources: "Everyone is conscious of the fact that in some areas of the world there is an explosive type of population increase, unsupportable, in that it is outdistancing food, it retards economic development. . . . What we are attempting to do, of course, is to encourage countries to curtail the rate of growth."[138] Indeed, the *Washington Post* reported that he viewed the problem as akin to the threat of nuclear war—a problem so serious, in fact, that governments would need to take official action to limit births. "It may need to be taken out of the voluntary category," Dr. Guttmacher said.[139]

Fears about so-called overpopulation have proved groundless (not least when it comes to global climate change, given that countries with rising birthrates are populated largely by poor people of color who contribute virtually nothing to the problem[140]), and we at least claim to be a society that values the lives of the disabled and unwanted. But that has not stopped the concerns of the early 1970s from driving the abortion debate today. Many abortion rights activists reject the twenty-week abortion bans passed in several US states (despite their relative popularity[141]) precisely because it will limit access to abortion targeted at disabled populations who are often not discovered to be disabled until after this stage of pregnancy.[142] Prenatal children with Down syndrome are at high risk given that, when they are discovered to have this particular disability, somewhere between two in three and nine in ten are killed via abortion precisely because of their disability. (This, even though they are likely to be happier with their lives than those who don't have Down syndrome.[143])

Politicians who support abortion rights today often say all the right things when it comes to their concern for women, but at times the mask slips and their full motivations become clear. During one of the 2019 debates leading up to the selection of a Democratic nominee for president, Senator Bernie Sanders of Vermont was asked if he would take on the challenges posed by global population growth. This was his response:

SANDERS: Well, Martha, the answer is yes. And the answer has everything to do with the fact that women in the United States of America, by the way, have a right to control their own bodies and make reproductive decisions.[144]

Remarkably, Sanders admitted in front of a national audience that he supported a woman's "right to choose" because of his concerns about population growth. Pro-lifers predictably balked at Sanders's statement, but otherwise his answer hardly made a wave.

Most social movements to have fewer babies, especially fewer disabled babies, are related to concerns about scarce resources. Sanders's questioner in the debate prefaced her question by claiming, "The planet cannot sustain this growth." The implication is that we simply don't have enough stuff (food, energy, tax revenue, infrastructure, etc.) to deal with increasing numbers of people, especially if they are disabled. But at times, as we saw in Schwartz's article above, the connection between abortion and resource concerns is even more direct.

After his death, a former abortion doctor in South Bend, Indiana, made headlines when authorities found the body parts of thousands of prenatal human beings in his home, garage, and car. As those who had had interactions with Dr. Klopfer were interviewed for the many news stories covering this gruesome discovery, we learned how he treated the *post*-natal human beings who entered his clinic. A Black woman whose previous abortion in his clinic left her wounded and bleeding, for instance, reported that when she hesitated to follow through on a plan to abort her twins (she was desperate because her partner had abandoned her and she was without resources), Dr. Klopfer pressured her into doing it anyway. According to reporting from CBS News Chicago he said, "If you don't do this, it will cost you . . . $240,000 to take care of a kid. So would you rather deal with that or would you rather go home and just go back to your regular life?"[145]

Such appeals to economic pressure for the necessity of abortion are anything but isolated. Indeed, in *Roe's* 1992 successor case, *Planned Parenthood v. Casey*, the Supreme Court's opinion seems cut from the same cloth as Dr. Klopfer's remarks:

> For two decades of economic and social developments, people have organized intimate relationships and made choices that define their views of themselves and their places in society, in reliance on the availability of abortion in the event that contraception should fail. The ability of women to participate equally in the economic and social life of the Nation has been facilitated by their ability to control their reproductive lives.[146]

Nearly twenty years after *Roe*, the Supreme Court of the United States abandoned much of its original legal framework and upheld the right to abortion based explicitly on concerns related to economics and resources.

Marginalizing Prenatal Human Beings

Let us recall once again that the fundamental human equality of human beings with catastrophic brain injuries was rejected in favor of what were considered other, more significant concerns. This chapter has shown that, in the case of prenatal children, their fundamental human equality obstructed concerns deemed more significant as well. And as happened with brain death, a new moral and legal vision was created which denied that prenatal human beings could have the same moral and legal value as the rest of us.

Indeed, before *Roe* made it illegal for US states to offer broad protections for prenatal human beings within the law, it was commonly done. Forsythe points out that the very state laws against abortion in Texas and Georgia that were challenged in *Roe* and *Doe* were part of their criminal code, which meant they were considered crimes against human life. The Georgia statute was amended in 1968 to refer to the "unborn child" and required a death certificate if he or she were killed via abortion. Forsythe also points out that "Anglo-American law has called the unborn child an 'unborn child' or a 'child' from at least the 1200s, a tradition that was inherited from Roman law." Everyone from Sir Edward Coke to William Blackstone to Oliver Wendell Holmes used the word "child" to refer to what today we call a "fetus."

However, we don't always use the term "fetus." Though we do so in the contexts of academic biology or abortion, in virtually every other context we use language that signals fundamental human equality. When the prenatal child is wanted, we speak about baby bumps, baby showers, babies kicking, and parents being told that their babies are healthy. When the child is unwanted we switch our language so that a human being can be more easily discarded as a mere object, with terms like "fetus," "product of conception," and even "parasite." *Roe* used the odd phrase "potential life." How many readers have heard a pregnant woman say, "Want to come over here and feel the potential life kicking?" Indeed, what *potential* life could move around in the first place? When I went to see the OB-GYN when my wife was pregnant with our son, Thaddeus, he never once said, "Good news, your potential life is really healthy and doing great!" Even as an abortion activist, Norma McCorvey talked about the fact that she was pregnant with a "baby." It turns out that in many contexts we use language which affirms equality and avoids the relatively new trend of selectively speaking about a "fetus." Previous chapters have noted how formerly-common ways of speaking have been twisted into incoherent knots as we are pushed to violate fundamental human equality. It shouldn't be surprising, therefore, that widely-legal abortion—which also violates fundamental human equality—uses twisted and at times totally incoherent language.

The previous two chapters focused on how new calls for personhood based mostly on a particular human being's capacity for consciousness have undermined fundamental human equality. Recall that even Joseph Fins, despite his profoundly countercultural fight for the civil rights of people with serious brain injuries, still focused on consciousness. Only human beings with the potential for consciousness, in his view, have the moral, social, and legal equality that comes with personhood. That's why it is so important for him that these populations get proper diagnostic tests and therapies. If his views were followed consistently on abortion, however, the prenatal human child would also be treated as a person only in light of her potential for consciousness (or rationality, moral capacity, autonomy, etc.), with no need to appeal to the nature of human beings.

On the other hand, rejecting Fins's view and arguing that potential is irrelevant[147] leaves us with a class of children who, though living members of the species *Homo sapiens*, are denied the fundamental equality of persons. And of course, if the potential of the prenatal child is rejected as irrelevant (in other words, if it only matters whether they have consciousness, rationality, etc., now, not whether they will have it in the future), then the potential of other human beings must be rejected as irrelevant. This would include not only the brain-damaged human beings for whom Fins is claiming equal treatment in the clinic; it would also include newborn human children as well. As Peter Singer and others have pointed out, these immature human beings are no more rational, self-aware, or autonomous than a snail or other similar creature. While newborns may be biologically human, they are not alive in a biographical sense and do not count as persons to Singer and others. Indeed, Singer is keen to point out that in the ancient world—before Christian ethics came to shape the West—there was no moral difference between abortion and infanticide. Only when Christianity came on the scene was fundamental human equality applied to both neonatal and prenatal human beings. The *Didache*, one of the earliest documents from the ancient Christian Church, explicitly forbids abortion and infanticide together. Given what we've just seen, it is perfectly consistent that, in a social context dominated by secularized and even irreligious rejections of the fundamental human equality at the heart of a Christian ethic, there is no justification for newborn human babies being counted the same as the rest of us. It isn't being a human being that matters. It is being a human being with certain actualized capacities or abilities that matters.

To some this may seem far-fetched. And while the secularized West isn't quite ready to join Singer and thinkers like him in explicitly saying that newborn children aren't the equal of other human beings, the groundwork has been laid to do precisely that. Keep in mind that very immature human beings born early (say, after twenty-four or twenty-five weeks of gestation) in the NICU are actually at the same stage of development as Norma's baby was when she was still trying to seek an abortion after the Texas court's ruling. Currently, the Democratic Party in the United States has rejected any legal standing for prenatal children at any stage of development,[148] which is consistent with a broader rejection of fundamental human equality. But if a prenatal human child at six months (or even older) doesn't have such equality, how long can it be pretended that a preterm human child born at six months does have such equality? Eventually, US practices and law will be pushed to be consistent.[149] In what may constitute a peek at attitudes toward which our culture is slouching, a recent study found a revealing fact about the views of health-care professionals in Flanders, Belgium: 89.1 percent agreed that "in the event of a serious (non-lethal) neonatal condition, administering drugs with the explicit intention to end neonatal life was acceptable."[150]

One of my deep frustrations with many in the traditional pro-life movement is that over the years we have often spoken about the prenatal child as if the pregnant mother to whom she is attached doesn't exist. We make the same mistake when we speak about the pregnant mother as if her prenatal child doesn't exist. We must instead do our level best to protect the fundamental human equality of both. Pro-lifers, led by the example of pro-life feminists, are increasingly interested in supporting women's equality by making sure women have the social and economic support necessary to bear and raise a child. They have long been on the front lines, providing information and resources— sometimes even housing—to women in difficult circumstances. They are also increasingly likely to support policies like increased job protections, generous child tax credits, and even government-supported paid family leave.[151]

But pro-life feminists also insist that whatever we do to support women must not come at the expense of the fundamental equality of other vulnerable populations. Doing so would violate any recognizable social justice approach. The pro-life activist group New Wave Feminists puts it well when they say that if "our liberation costs innocent lives, it is merely oppression redistributed."[152] According to pro-life feminists, it is offensive and deeply anti-woman to suggest that women can have social and economic lives equal to men's only by pitting themselves violently against the equal dignity of their prenatal children. This preserves a patriarchal social order made for people who do not get pregnant. For instance, in a recent exposé the *New York Times* found that pregnancy discrimination against women at work was "rampant inside America's biggest companies."[153] Childcare is hopelessly expensive, especially for vulnerable single women, and the United States is the only country in the developed world that does not offer women mandatory paid family leave.

Our culture of abortion rights and rejection of the fundamental human equality of the prenatal human child is set up to benefit those who do not get pregnant. Given this context, is it any wonder that the dignity of Norma McCorvey and her needs as a struggling and desperate pregnant woman were ignored? That she was used by others as a pawn, as a mere means to some other end? Or that in 1973, men decided *Roe v. Wade* on the basis of protecting the overwhelmingly male profession of medicine? Or that in *Casey* the Supreme Court would maintain the right to abortion because it is necessary for women to continue to play a game rigged in favor of men?

Given these realities, it is more important than ever that more and more Christian pro-lifers refuse to choose between the fundamental human equality of the mother and her child. I found it very hopeful, for instance, that as I was writing the first draft of this chapter the 2020 March for Life in Washington, D.C., was approaching. Its theme? "Life Empowers: Pro-Life is Pro-Woman."[154]

Conclusion

Abortion has so infected the United States' political culture that it is rightly referred to as our second civil war. A cold civil war, but a civil war nonetheless. The confirmations of Brett Kavanaugh and Amy Coney Barrett to the Supreme Court have generated bitter political arguments, the heart of the conflict being over abortion. As we saw in previous chapters, abortion politics and law often have deep connections with certain cases that, at first glance, seem to have little to do with abortion itself. But for many of those who seek to continue the secularization of medicine and medical ethics, abortion rights lie at the heart of what they most want to protect. And often they have good reasons for such concerns: the equal dignity of women in vulnerable situations should be kept at the very center of who we are. But we must absolutely refuse to think of dignity and equality as a zero-sum game where one population can be treated equally only at the expense of another. Even the complex arguments to be had about abortion in the case of sexual violence or when the mother's health is in danger (and I think such arguments do have merit) should be conducted in ways that do not discard the fundamental human equality of the prenatal child. Prenatal children must not be erased from the abortion debate, nor should their mothers.

Given a central theme of this book, it is worth noting again at the conclusion of this chapter how much the concern for protecting a secularized and irreligious medical field was and is at the heart of the protection of the right to abortion. Instead of feminist and other women-centered folks working together for reasonable laws to protect and support both vulnerable populations, we instead have a toxic political discourse in which a major US political party advocates for virtually no legal limits on a physician's decision. But as we have seen and will see throughout this book, investing such moral authority in protecting what physicians do misunderstands the kind of training and expertise they have—and risks capitulating to a privileged and utilitarian idea of which human beings' lives have value. The abortion rate for babies with Down syndrome is so high, for example, in part because in these situations physicians and other health-care providers use directive and ableist language to persuade (and even coerce[155]) women into having abortions.

Abortion is a particularly important issue where those of us who stand for fundamental human equality must be strong and not let ourselves be bullied out of the debate. Politically speaking, at least, this third major way in which fundamental human equality has been undermined seems to be of greatest consequence and is the point around which the general arguments raised in this book seem to pivot. For centuries now, activists pushing for justice for X vulnerable population have been told by their detractors that the full inclusion of X as our moral and legal equals would lead to all kinds of terrible consequences for our society. We've seen this tactic when X = women, people of color, immigrants, religious minorities, gays and lesbians, and others. In an attempt to keep X from achieving fundamental human equality, scary stories are often told about what will happen to another often legitimately vulnerable population. But these scare tactics are almost never borne out by the evidence. When it comes to abortion, for instance, the rhetoric on what happens to women if prenatal human beings are given legal protections is directly contradicted by the examples of Chile and (until recently) Ireland. Both countries banned almost all abortions and actually had better health outcomes for women than their abortion-permissive neighbors.[156] In the case of Chile, outcomes for women actually improved when they protected their prenatal children with the law.

Simply put, the equal dignity of every human being—because they are created in the image and likeness of God—should never be compromised. We can and should debate *what that equal dignity means*, especially in complex cases, but we should never abandon every human being's fundamental equality. That said, as the irreligious forces of inequality grow more numerous, powerful, and bold, it is more and more difficult to stand up in this way. The case of our next chapter, Alfie Evans, and the topic of neurodegenerative disease in toddlers demonstrate this struggle in spades.

Chapter Five

Alfie Evans and Neurodegenerative Disease

The Story of Alfie Evans

Pope Francis pleaded with a doctor to do whatever was possible "and impossible!" to bring a very sick British toddler named Alfie Evans to Bambino Gesù Hospital in Rome.[157] The doctor to whom he was appealing was Mariella Enoc, president of the hospital; the pope asked her to fly to England and bring back the remarkable little boy and get him the care his parents desperately sought for him. All costs of transport and treatment would be covered by Bambino Gesù.[158]

The stakes were high and the drama was intense. In addition to a pope who very publicly (via his Twitter account[159]) rejected the views of the United Kingdom's medical and legal establishment, the story included two young, religious, working-class British parents fighting for their son against a privileged class with a very different understanding of the good. Alfie's British doctors, you see, didn't think he was benefiting from the medical care keeping him alive and wanted it removed. This standoff generated an international tidal wave of debate over what should be done. Alfie was given emergency Italian citizenship and an air ambulance was scrambled to take him to Rome. A German physician, also willing to care for Alfie, warned of the return of a dangerous ableism that had infamously plagued vulnerable populations in his own country within living memory. Alfie's parents filed for an emergency writ of *habeas corpus* to release their son from what they said was unlawful detention in the hospital. Alfie continued to breathe after British medicine and law, over the objections of his parents, managed to have his ventilator removed. After continuing to breathe for the better part of five days, at 2:30 AM on April 28, 2018, Alfie, to use the words of his father, "lay down his shield and gained his wings."

How did the story come to this dramatic point? Within the first few months of his life, Alfie developed an unknown and devastating neurodegenerative disease. It destroyed, his physicians said, most of his brain—including the thalami, which regulate the pathways of the brain and control the stimuli to the most basic sensory functions. They said Alfie lost the capacity to hear, see, smell, or respond to touch, other than reflexively.[160] They further claimed he was in a "semi-vegetative state" and could not breathe on his own. His medical team maintained a view that was upheld by the UK Supreme Court: there was no hope of his ever getting better and therefore it was in Alfie's best interest to be extubated, given palliative care, and allowed to die.[161]

But Alfie and his father were baptized Catholics and the family utterly rejected this line of reasoning. They used every legal and social means available to give their son the chance to fight for however long he had fight in him. As Catholic teaching demands, they refused the idea that one should aim at the death of an innocent person, even by omission. Alfie's father even flew to the Vatican for a twenty-minute meeting with the pope—after which Alfie was made an emergency Italian citizen, Bambino Gesù Hospital made it clear they wanted to care for Alfie, and Pope Francis made an urgent public appeal to let his parents bring him to Rome.

If things didn't work out in Italy, Alfie and his parents also had the option to seek care in Germany. Indeed, Alfie's parents invoked the expert testimony of Munich physician Dr. Nikolaus Haas, who specializes in pediatric intensive care. If Alfie were transported to Munich, Dr. Haas said, the plan "would include an estimated 14 days stay at our PICU including a tracheostomy and PEG insertion, a repeat EEG monitoring and MRI of the brain, equipment with a home ventilation system including training of the parents and a dedicated neuropaediatric assessment and potentially additional genetic testing."[162] While Dr. Haas agreed that at this point the progressive neurological disorder would likely lead to Alfie's death, the boy had already lived longer than his UK medical team expected, and with the proper treatment and care had an unknown amount of time he could spend with his parents and family. Withdrawing treatment, said Dr. Haas, was "certainly not" in Alfie's best interest. Instead, it was clearly better for him to live "the possibly short rest of his life in dignity together with his family if this is the wish of his parents at home." In addition, said Dr. Haas, a "dedicated neurological rehabilitation institution may be of additional benefit because there may well be other treatment and stimulation therapies I am not aware of."

But then Dr. Haas dropped the hammer on the doctors and judges who wanted to remove treatment:

> Because of our history in Germany, we've learned that there are some things you just don't do with severely handicapped children. A society must be prepared to look after these severely handicapped children and not decide that life support has to be withdrawn against the will of the parents if there is uncertainty of the feelings of the child, as in this case.

Justice Hayden of the Liverpool High Court never explained why he dismissed Dr. Haas's words as "inflammatory and inappropriate," but his reaction bears a striking resemblance to reactions we saw in chapter 3 to claims about the moral requirements to respect the dignity of severely disabled patients like Terri Schiavo. The gap between the two conflicting understandings of the good is so wide that one side cannot understand the other as doing anything other than inappropriately inflaming the debate.

At any rate, despite the options to go to Italy or Germany, the medical and legal powers in the United Kingdom held Alfie Evans under armed guard and had his ventilator removed despite his parents' protests. But little Alfie, fighting for his life, refused to stop breathing. The hospital, however, did not immediately provide oxygen for him—with the result that his parents gave their son mouth-to-mouth aid to help get oxygen into his lungs.[163] Eventually, the hospital did provide oxygen and for days Alfie breathed on his own. All this time, an air ambulance was waiting to take Alfie to a hospital that would give him the help he needed; international frustration mounted. The president of Italy's National Institutes of Health, for instance, criticized the rigidity of the United Kingdom's National Health Service as "shocking and inhumane."[164]

And then Alfie died. Despite an international debate about what was going on in his brain, no autopsy was performed. His death did not stop the acrimony and his story will be discussed and debated for decades to come. And as we will see toward the end of this chapter, his struggle and that of his family may not have been in vain. Though multiple sides accuse their opponents of manipulating a little boy for their own agenda, it may be that the ethical issues raised in the debate over his case have put the United Kingdom on a different path. But let's put that aside for the moment and analyze closely what was going on in this case.

Moral Analysis of Alfie's Case

The first thing to mention, especially given what we saw in chapter 3, is that labeling Alfie Evans as in a "semi-vegetative" state was perhaps even less helpful than being labeled as just plain "vegetative." What we thought we knew about people deemed to be in such a state—and about their potential for getting better—has turned out to be almost totally wrong. And it may well have been wrong regarding what we thought was going on with Alfie as well. The disease the little boy had was never identified; various therapies were never attempted to coax him back to consciousness. The conclusion of the UK medical and legal community that the brain "simply has no capacity to regenerate itself" is contradicted by the story of Maggie, whose brain, as we saw in chapter 3, did precisely that—and she regained consciousness and the ability to communicate. Given the massive backtrack that has had to be made on vegetative patients, we should hesitate to make broad proclamations that patients like Alfie "will never do X" and that there is "no hope" for recovery—especially when such proclamations are used to take the decision out of the hands of those who care about them the most.

Consider, for instance, the case of baby Noah, a boy with fluid in his brain that had destroyed all but 2% of healthy brain tissue. Doctors advised Noah's parents to abort. The parents rejected that advice but did buy a coffin, expecting to use it soon after his birth. But three years later Noah "shocked doctors after scans showed his brain had almost full function."[165] Furthermore, some human beings whose cerebral cortex has been destroyed still know who they are, crack jokes, and can point themselves out in pictures.[166] It might have also been the case that the drugs Alfie was taking were actually hiding thalamic connections in his brain,[167] but again, an autopsy wasn't done so we can't be sure. Here's the bottom line: we just aren't sure about a lot of things related to what we think we know about the brain and how what we think we know relates to the (current and/ or future) consciousness of a patient with a devastating neurological disease or injury.

Let's set this (major) issue aside and for the sake of argument assume that the medical judgment that Alfie would never recover and (after an undetermined amount of time) would die of his unexplained neurodegenerative disease was correct. Apart from his neurological disease, Alfie was actually a fairly robust and healthy human being. We've already seen that he defied the expectations of his medical team. After being extubated he fought for life by breathing for days. His UK doctors also thought he wouldn't survive a bad case of pneumonia prior to that, but Alfie fought off the infection like a champ. As with the cases we've examined in the previous chapters, Justice Hayden and others who wanted Alfie's ventilator removed were not driven by the common humanity they shared with the little boy. Though at one point the judge did offhandedly admit that a living human being like Alfie has intrinsic value, he never factored that detail into his ultimate decision. He instead focused on "the nature and severity of the child's underlying condition" which "may make it difficult or impossible for [him] to enjoy the benefits that continued life brings."[168]

Considering what we have seen about changes in the medical community over the last few decades, it should be no surprise that this understanding of the value of human life—one that rejects the notion of fundamental equality for all—came from the guidance given by The Royal College of Paediatrics and Child Health. As my colleague in moral theology Matthew Shadle points out, the understanding that Alfie's life is valuable only if he (based on a particular understanding of the good) "derives benefit" from it excludes the idea that there is value in life itself.[169] But fundamental human equality relies on the idea that human life itself is a good that should be respected in every circumstance, no matter how certain humans differ with regard to cognitive ability, sex/gender, social class, race, and similar factors.

As we discussed in chapter 3, life-sustaining treatment certainly can be removed while maintaining respect for the equal dignity of human beings. First, though it might be foreseen that death is likely, it cannot be intended that death come about (either by an action or omission). Second, it must be reasonably determined that the burden of the medical treatment is disproportionate with respect to any expected benefit. At times Justice Hayden and others seemed concerned about the burden of the ventilator on Alfie, and this is perfectly legitimate. The ventilator could be withdrawn precisely as part of what is necessary to respect Alfie's equal dignity and worth as a human being.

But in this case there are multiple reasons to think this is not what was going on. For starters, Justice Hayden cited physicians who claimed that Alfie's neural degeneration was such that he no longer responded to "painful stimuli." Elsewhere he cited medical claims that what appeared to be reactions to "pain stimulation like pinching" were due to spinal reflexes or seizures. Alfie, his physicians said, didn't respond neurologically to such painful stimuli, and they made this a major part of their case for his complete neurological devastation. So the primary concern couldn't have been about the pain or other burden of the medical treatment, either in the clinic or in the air ambulance that would have taken him to Rome or Munich. Indeed, the medical guidance used by Justice Hayden says that "even in the absence of demonstrable pain or suffering continuation of [ventilation] may not be in their best interests because it cannot provide overall benefit."

So, morally speaking, how should we describe the action that was taken in removing Alfie's ventilator? Even if it was about removing burdensome treatment, the benefit of Alfie's continued life itself didn't play a role in the decision. (This is an important reason why it should have been Alfie's parents, and not secularized and—as we will see below—irreligious folks weighing the benefits and burdens.) But if it was about the burden of ventilation, and Alfie's life was considered the equal of every other human life, then we should have expected his medical team and the UK justice system to react with joy and rush to support Alfie's life when he started to breathe on his own after the burdensome treatment was removed. But that's not what happened. Again, Alfie's parents saw that he was not getting enough oxygen and gave him mouth-to-mouth aid themselves. According to their legal team, the hospital withdrew ventilation at 9:20 PM and it wasn't until 4:00 or 5:00 AM the next day that the hospital "reluctantly gave in to continued requests and provided some hydration and oxygen support."[170] This was only after what Alfie's father described as a "lengthy talk" with the medical team in which he pleaded with them to provide his son oxygen.[171]

Those who advocate for personal equality, as opposed to human equality, often claim that equality is indicated by traits strongly connected with the ability to enjoy the benefits continued life brings: self-awareness, consciousness, autonomy, volitional action, etc. Justice Hayden and the medical team were not concerned with the burden of the treatment, but with the effect Alfie's profound disability would likely have on his ability to derive such benefits from life. They withdrew treatment not "merely foreseeing" that Alfie would die, but rather intending that he die. They kept Alfie's parents from seeking out other health-care teams that would treat Alfie, not because they were concerned about how Alfie might experience a short trip in the air ambulance, but because they thought it was in Alfie's best interest to die. The position of some who opposed his parents—that it would be better for Alfie to die under armed guard in a UK hospital, than to *risk* death on the air ambulance while fighting for his life—makes no sense. No, just as with Jahi and Terri, Alfie's treatment was removed because those who had power over him decided that it was in his best interest to die.

But what kind of being died when Alfie Evans died? For Jahi and Terri, many explicitly said that, though a living human body might be present, they were no longer there as persons. Because no one explicitly stated that Alfie (clearly a human being who fought off dangerous lung infections, breathed on his own, maintained homeostasis, and more) was no longer a person, there seem to be two different moral possibilities concerning this question. In the first option, Alfie is seen as a disabled person, fundamentally equal to the rest of us, who needs to be killed because in the judgment of able-bodied people his disability makes his life of no net benefit to him. In the second option, Alfie is a living human being but no longer a person equal in dignity to the rest of us because he is not conscious, not rational, not autonomous, and has no potential ever to be so again. In which case the medical team was aiming at the death of a human being, but not at the death *of a person.*

It is possible that some of those responsible for Alfie's extubation may have had the first option in mind, but as I've argued elsewhere, this opens the door for able-bodied people holding positions of power in the state to aim at the death of other disabled children because they judge that the children's lives are of no net benefit to them.[172] Upon further reflection, especially given the emphasis on Alfie's being in a "semi-vegetative state" and having lost (in the view of his physicians) all potential for morally meaningful capacities, I think it is more likely that they thought Alfie was no longer a person like you or me. At the very least, given the secularized framework in which they were operating, there was no consistent way to argue that Jahi and Terri were no longer persons, yet Alfie was still a person. The logic and reasoning which arrives at the non-personhood of human beings who are brain dead or in a vegetative state also arrives at the non-personhood of "semi-vegetative" human beings like Alfie Evans.

Irreligion Arrives in Earnest

Unsurprisingly, deeply religious people who want to defend fundamental human equality—like Alfie's parents, their legal team, and their supporters around the world—made their objections to the decision of his medical team quite public. Based on their understanding of the good, they saw Alfie being unlawfully detained with the goal of aiming at his death because his disability made him unworthy of life. How could they not speak up in the strongest possible terms? But when they did so, they provoked a reaction that turned the Alfie Evans case into a paradigmatic example of the hostile secularizing and irreligious trends highlighted throughout this book.

I make this point in some detail in an article I wrote for the *Journal of Medicine and Philosophy* (JMP).[173] Recall from chapter 1 that the secularizing and irreligious trends in medicine and medical ethics marginalize religious visions of the good as biased, while (often uncritically) accepting their own version of the good as objective and fact-based. Udo Schuklenk wrote an editorial on Alfie's case for the journal *Bioethics* in which he criticized the negative response from religious thinkers as "ideological." This response, it is implied, is in opposition to the supposed non-ideological and fact-based approach of the UK medical and legal establishment. Indeed, Justice Hayden was able to find as a matter of "fact" that it was in Alfie's best interest to have treatment withdrawn and to die. (This greatly complicated the appeals process because under the UK legal system such findings of fact cannot be appealed.) But there isn't anything like objective medical or legal fact to be discovered so as to demonstrate Alfie's best interests in this case. There are only judgments based on deeply contested visions of the good.

When Paul Diamond, legal counsel for Alfie Evans's family, filed for a writ of *habeas corpus* based on concerns and reasoning that are at the heart of this book, Justice Hayden repeatedly slapped him down for offering the court "ridiculous emotive nonsense."[174] In my JMP article I note with interest that in his ruling Hayden ominously claimed that he was "very much aware" that the family was committed to Roman Catholicism. He dismissed arguments from the Christian Legal Centre as "vituperation and bile." One of their Catholic counselors was singled out as a "fanatical and deluded young man" with a "malign hand." Upon appeal, Justice McFarlane said there had been a "darker side" to the support Alfie's parents had received, warning that their vulnerability had been exploited by Christian pro-life groups. (As we will see below, because of the Evans's working-class status the UK medical and legal establishment condescended to them like this multiple times.) Chapter 1 called out Murphy's irreligious bioethics for refusing to reflect on the actual arguments of one's presumed opposition. It is enough, in his view, simply to claim that the arguments of religious people lack objectivity and are prone to ideological excess, and so should be dismissed. This kind of irreligious approach prevented Alfie's parents from having their arguments taken seriously.

My article also showed how the major media covering and commenting on the case were nearly unhinged in their irreligiosity, citing alarmist quotes like the following—which was fairly typical—to explain where severe criticism of the UK's medical and legal establishment was coming from:

> The Guardian has learned that an international network of Catholic fundamentalists has played a growing role in advising Alfie's parents, including organising Evans' audience with the pope last week, arranging a string of medical experts to assess Alfie, and replacing the family's Liverpool-based legal team with the anti-LGBT Christian Legal Centre this month.[175]

The *Daily Mail* insisted that Alfie was "a tragic pawn in a religious war" in a case that had been "hijacked by the Catholic Church."[176] A *Daily Mirror* headline claimed that the "Christians hijacking Alfie Evans' last days are evil incarnate." The piece referred to them as "bandwagon bandits who have leapt on his tragedy to push religious fundamentalism down our throats."[177] We also saw the classic irreligious canard of ostensibly trying to make sure "reason can still prevail over white-hot emotion" and "for evidence to be considered on its merits"—without advancing one's "own beliefs" and certainly not those "of organized religion."[178] But as should be more than clear at this point in the book, on the issues at stake in the case of Alfie Evans there is no view from nowhere. Everyone brought their own ideology and beliefs (not to mention "white-hot emotion") to bear in discussions about what was best for this little boy. There is no place of neutral rationality when it comes to clashes of different understandings of the good.

Often, those who stand outside the situation are best able to see how ideology is functioning. Dr. Enoc, president of the hospital in Rome that wanted to treat Alfie, said that the hostile reaction in the United Kingdom to the possibility of transport to Italy was "a response to an ideological battle." Noting that the judge's reasoning went well beyond strict legal interpretation, she claimed that the United Kingdom's rejection of Alfie's traveling to Italy was based in part on "hostility to the Vatican hospital."[179] One does not have to read too deeply between the lines to pick up on the anti-religious and anti-Catholic aspect she thinks was central to the decision. Think for a moment about how hostile, how dismissive those who had power over Alfie had to be of his parents' position in order to take the decision out of their hands. Essentially, they had to believe that Alfie's parents were proposing a kind of child abuse; that is the only legitimate reason for the state to detain a child this way.

The events surrounding the case of Alfie Evans make it clear not only how irreligion has arrived in earnest, but also how it can become a dominating force.

Social Factors as Threats to Human Equality

As with the cases and examples from previous chapters, multiple social factors contributed to undermining Alfie's fundamental human equality—including concern over scarce medical resources and biased perspectives based on social class. Allocation of scarce medical resources was not explicitly stated as part of the decision not to treat Alfie, but significant indirect evidence suggests that it played a role, especially early on. When discussing a possible trip to Germany in his ruling, for instance, Justice Hayden randomly included the cost of Alfie's treatment there: "Based on the German hospital payment system these estimated costs would be about 65.000 €uro [*sic*] for the 14 days including surgery. Additional cost offers can be obtained for transport and home ventilation equipment."

A single-payer health system like the United Kingdom's National Health Service (NHS) requires explicit and difficult judgments about how to spend finite resources. An NHS office, the National Institute for Health and

Care Excellence, gives guidance for using medicines and treatment. Called NICE for short, it explicitly says that it is concerned with "how well the medicine or treatment works in relation to how much it costs the NHS—does it represent value for money?"[180] NICE generally uses a metric called a Quality-Adjusted Life Year (QALY) to judge whether a treatment or intervention's cost can be justified. NICE defines the concept this way:

> One QALY is equal to 1 year of life in perfect health. QALYs are calculated by estimating the years of life remaining for a patient following a particular treatment or intervention and weighting each year with a quality-of-life score (on a 0 to 1 scale). It is often measured in terms of the person's ability to carry out the activities of daily life, and freedom from pain and mental disturbance.[181]

NICE is aware that using QALYs is controversial but justifies it by noting that there is no uncontroversial way to make decisions about allocating scarce medical resources, and this is what they have decided to use.[182] (It should go without saying that a decision to use QALYs is based on a particular understanding of the good, not objective medical science.) To apply it to our concerns in this chapter, suppose NICE claimed Alfie had zero ability to "carry out the activities of daily life." Though there is apparently much confusion about how to use QALYs in such a circumstance,[183] they would presumably multiply by zero however many months or years they estimate he is likely to survive on a ventilator to determine the amount of money they should spend on his care. (Especially, but not only, if it involved new or experimental treatments or therapies.) That would of course be no money at all. But suppose a more generous quality-of-life evaluation gave Alfie a 0.1 rating instead of 0.0. If they also generously estimated that he could live five more years on a ventilator, that would give him 0.5 QALYs. And because NICE wants treatments to be at or below 20,000 euros per QALY (anything beyond that requires approval for an exception), even in this generous judgment the guidelines would only permit 10,000 euros for his care.

Given that this is how the NHS operates on a regular basis,[184] and that it helps form basic assumptions about how health care is delivered in the United Kingdom, it is reasonably likely that the NICE office had these considerations somewhere between the back and front of their minds when the courts were asked to overrule the request of Alfie's parents that he continue to be treated. Eventually the case became about a clash of ideologies (Bambino Gesù was going to pay for everything, so in that case, cost wasn't an issue), but at first, at least, it was overwhelmingly likely that what one might call a "QALY mentality" played a significant role in the NHS's decision to overrule the parents and remove Alfie's ventilator. It is little wonder why the National Council on Independent Living, Not Dead Yet, and the Autistic Self Advocacy Network recently adopted a strong resolution against using QALYs in the United States.[185]

Another factor that appears to have played a role here is social class. Especially when considering which points of view are rational and defensible versus those deemed irrational and emotional, the views of high-class folks with power generally end up in the first category while the views of minorities and the working classes are generally in the second. This was evident at several points throughout the ordeal: Alfie's family was working class and Justice Hayden drew attention to this (both directly and indirectly) at multiple points in the legal proceedings and even in the text of his official ruling:

> Alfie's mother was then 18 years old and this was her first pregnancy. Alfie's father Tom was 19 years of age. Though self-evidently very young and though Alfie had not been planned his parents were delighted by him.

What possible relevance could the age of his parents or whether they "planned" to have Alfie have for this case? Noting this information makes sense only if one desires to locate Alfie's parents publicly as members of a social class that typically gets married and has (unplanned) children at much younger ages than do higher class Brits. It is not a coincidence that the idea that certain traits and capabilities make a human being a person with fundamental equality comes from people of privilege and higher social classes.

Hayden was also clearly not expecting Alfie's parents to be so well versed in the medical science surrounding the case. Consider this remarkable passage—again, from the judge's official ruling—about Alfie's father:

> His knowledge of the paperwork and the medical records was prodigious. His understanding

of the functioning of the brain and his exploration of competing hypotheses was remarkable. At one point in the evidence when he had asked a question of particular complexity I asked him if somebody had been providing the questions for him. He told me, entirely convincingly, that he had written it out a moment or two before. His uncle, sitting next to him, confirmed it. [Alfie's father] left school at 16. He served an apprenticeship as a plasterer. It says much about his commitment to his son and the time and energy he has directed to this case that he has absorbed the issues so completely and intelligently.

Again, none of this had anything to do with the legal issues before the court, but now we know that Alfie's father dropped out of school early and was earning a living doing manual labor.

The Supreme Court's ruling went further, dismissing Alfie's parents in ways that are as shocking as they are revolting. In response to their request to travel with Alfie to Italy or Germany, Lady Justice King—in a series of claims that are nearly unthinkable without a monstrous bias related to social class—said the following:

It is clear and understandable that they have been unable to think through the disadvantages for them as a family to relocating either to Italy or Munich without the support of their extended families and unable to speak either language, in order to be able to spend Alfie's last weeks or months in what they currently regard as a more empathetic environment.[186]

Maybe it is a result of living in the United States, a country built in large part by working-class people—often with small children—who arrived on our shores without knowing the language and seeking a more empathetic environment, but I cannot imagine how such class-based condescension and gross paternalism found its way into a serious legal judgment.

In a case like this, problems of class and privilege are made worse by the role doctors play. We've seen in previous chapters that highly educated physicians are also part of a privileged, high-class community with its own deep, mostly unconscious biases. I pointed out in chapter 2, for instance, that physicians consistently rate the quality of life of their patients lower than the patients themselves do. And when confronted with the fact that patients generally prefer length of life to quality of life, physicians admit, "We think we know what is best for a patient, but this is often wrong."[187] Americans should not spend too much time looking down our noses at the United Kingdom in this regard, however. While we would almost never explicitly or legally take the decision out of the hands of parents, I have pointed out elsewhere that a physician's desire to achieve the outcome he wants is sometimes so strong that he will engage in deceptive practices called "slow coding" or "show coding." This happens when physicians dishonestly agree with the parents that everything possible will be done for their child ("full code") but in reality the medical team decides on the down-low not to engage in aggressive treatment. Some ethicists today defend this practice in which physicians, often basing their judgment on their own vision of the good, determine that the low quality of a particular child's life makes that child not worth trying to save.[188]

After Alfie

Cases like Alfie's are hardly isolated events. In a similar case, Charlie Gard, another British boy with a neurodegenerative disease, was extubated despite his parents' having other treatment options overseas. He died a little less than a year before Alfie.[189] Indeed, Alfie's lawyers claim there have been twenty-two similar cases in the United Kingdom alone over the past five years.[190] To avoid international incidents of this kind in the future, there is growing support in multiple constituencies in the United Kingdom for legislation called "Charlie's Law." This law would permit parents to seek treatment at other hospitals unless it would cause the child significant harm. If the parents and NHS disagree about "significant harm," the hospital would be required to offer private mediation before asking for a legal ruling.[191]

As of the end of 2020 Charlie's Law had not yet been passed, but already there is evidence of a culture change. Five-year-old Tafida Raqeeb sustained a brain injury so serious that, according to the NHS hospital treating her, "she has no awareness and, with no prospect of recovery, life support should be withdrawn."[192] Like Alfie's parents, Tafida's are very religious—and they obtained a religious ruling from the Islamic Council of Europe that it would be a "great sin" and "absolutely impermissible" to consent to removing her life support.[193] Also like Alfie's parents, Tafida's parents managed to find a cost-free opportunity to travel to Italy for their child's treatment and argued in court that the NHS was detaining their child unlawfully. But unlike Alfie's case, the judge sided with the parents, not the hospital.[194] Though he was persuaded by medical opinion that Tafida's situation was "irreversible" and that medical treatment (which included a ventilator) imposed a large burden with virtually no or little benefit, Justice MacDonald nevertheless respected the fact that Tafida and her family were religious and gave weight specifically to their religious views about the sanctity of human life for its own sake.

Despite some dubious objections to this stance of respect for the views of religious people,[195] and fully acknowledging the unfortunate fact that a civil court, which has shown itself to be secularized and irreligious, again took it upon itself to determine a vision of the good for this religious family, this ruling was an astonishing and hopeful development. And there was more good news: just a few months after being transferred to a children's hospital in Genoa, Tafida was moved out of intensive care and into a rehabilitation unit.[196] As I write this, she is being liberated from her ventilator and can now breathe on her own for an hour at a time. Her Italian doctors say that "it is extremely difficult to understand her degree of participation in the environment" and that when there is doubt "we must always behave as if participation were greater than what we are able to perceive." They admit the relationship between neurological damage and future consciousness is murky, and are therefore "trying to give this little girl time to understand if there'll be a potential improvement." Humbly acknowledging the limitation of medicine in this area, they note that "much of that potential improvement is yet to be understood."

Conclusion

Suppose a new therapy is invented for Tafida that helps her recover consciousness over the next several months or years. (In light of what we learned in chapter 3 about what has happened to 20 percent of patients deemed vegetative after they received the correct therapies, this is not an outlandish proposition.) Would some physicians and bioethicists be forced to say that she was a nonperson before the therapy was invented and a person only after it was used? Such a claim is totally bizarre. Fundamental human equality doesn't come from the level of medical technology we happen to have readily available. Tafida remains the same human being throughout the process of her life: from prenatal child, to baby, to toddler, to a five-year-old with a devastating neurological injury, to (in this thought experiment) a seven-year-old with some level of consciousness. Human beings have the same dignified nature throughout their lives, regardless of their ability to express that nature at any particular moment. Our fundamental equality doesn't come from, say, having a particular percentage chance of being conscious in the future. It comes from having a nature in common that reflects the image and likeness of God. Tafida, even at her most disabled, has that nature in common with every reader of this book. Charlie Gard had that nature in common with every reader of this book. And Alfie Evans had that nature in common with every reader of this book.

But as many readers will know—tragically, often on the basis of experiences with family and friends—beyond the ultra-rare situations of Charlie and Alfie there are more frequent examples of neurodegenerative disease. In its late stages, Alzheimer's disease, for instance, can be similarly devastating to neurological capacity—and it affects human beings by the millions. Relatively common chromosomal and genetic disorders can also devastate the brain and disable human beings in such profound ways that, under certain views of personhood coming under scrutiny in this book, their fundamental human equality may be at risk. As the United States continues to deliver more and more health care via state governments with fixed budgets, and as a result more directly confronts the thorny and complex problems concerning how we spend limited health-care resources, the chances are ever higher that in the future there will be significant pressure to use few resources on those with profound disabilities.

Chapter Six

What's Next:
Late-Stage Dementia and Beyond

Peter Singer as Prophet and Mirror

Princeton University's Peter Singer is arguably the most influential philosopher of the last fifty years. He is certainly a contemporary prophet and activist on behalf of the secularized visions of the good that have undermined the religious foundations of fundamental human equality. We've discussed his views a few times in this book. He is particularly clear in showing that brain-dead human beings are in fact living human beings—with the goal of demonstrating that realizing this is a watershed moment for how we in the developed West think about moral status and value. By saying that living human beings can be killed for their vital organs, insists Singer, we have said quite clearly that what matters is being a person, not being a human being. He is absolutely right to name this shift in defining death as a watershed moment which began the process of a more foundational shift in our understanding of fundamental equality. Based on his vision of the good, it is a moment of triumph. A moment where we first successfully cut through the shackles of an intellectual tradition which, for the better part of two thousand years, focused on the inherent value of human beings.

I, of course, hold precisely the opposite view: that this fundamental shift is a terrible mistake, one which sets us on a path that has undermined human equality, sending to the margins some of the most vulnerable members of the human family, discarding them as mere things. As a side note, I used to think of Peter Singer as close to evil incarnate for being so mistaken on this question. But over the last several years I've come to see my view as deeply mistaken—not only because his views on the value of the ecological world and our duties to the poor have helped me reconnect to the radical position of my own Roman Catholic vision of the good on those issues,[197] but also because of his relentless focus on consistency in applying the first principles of his utilitarian understanding of the good. Indeed, he is virtually the only major public thinker who is forthright and clear about the implications of rejecting fundamental human equality. By holding a mirror up to our culture, he (perhaps incidentally) offers us the chance to pause and think about whether we actually want to become what we are becoming.

We've already seen, for instance, that Singer moves smoothly from the marginalization of prenatal human beings to the marginalization of newborn human beings. Both are fellow members of the species *Homo sapiens*, but to Singer both fail to count as persons—for the same reason that Jahi McMath, Terri Schiavo, and Alfie Evans fail to count as persons: newborn infants lack the requisite traits. If you are pro-choice on abortion because the fetus is not a person, argues Singer, then you should be pro-choice for infanticide as well because a newborn human baby is not a person either. If you are horrified by this position, as I am, it won't do simply to exclaim your horror and call him names. You need to make an argument. Singer is completely consistent in his viewpoint and rightly predicts what the future holds for newborn human infants if we stay on our current path. Don't blame the messenger. Singer is merely applying the central principles of a vision of the good broadly shared among those who hold with a secularized vision of medicine and bioethics. If we want to challenge the conclusions, we need to challenge the core vision of the good behind it.

As if arguing for infanticide weren't provocative enough, Singer has followed his first principles consistently to another conclusion many find horrific: namely, that human beings with end-stage dementia are also no longer persons and therefore do not share fundamental equality with the rest of us. Like living human beings who are brain dead, in a vegetative state, in a "semi-vegetative" state, or prenatal or neonatal, fellow members of *Homo sapiens* with late-stage dementia do not have rationality, self-awareness, or autonomy. They lack the ability to care about their lives and cannot have an interest in (and cannot benefit from) continued life. By Singer's account, a *human being* may be alive biologically, but biographically the *person* is no longer there. To use the words on Terri's gravestone: though a living body remains, they have "departed this earth."

Singer's conclusion became deeply relevant to a development in his own family. He had publicly argued that scarce health-care resources should be reserved for persons and withheld from human beings who were alive only in a biological sense. Some time after making this claim, however, his mother became precisely the kind of human non-person he was describing. Like many millions of others, in her late 60s Cora Singer developed dementia and lost her rationality and self-awareness. Singer is well known for living out his stated moral positions with a remarkable level of consistency—he is a very serious vegan and gives away more than 40 percent of his salary to address global poverty. But in this situation Singer could not maintain his consistency. Despite his stated point of view, he committed substantial financial resources to the care and treatment of his mother. When asked about this for a *New Yorker* story, he said, "Perhaps it is more difficult than I thought before, because it is different when it's your mother."[198]

Notice that he didn't say that in doing so he rejected the conclusion that his living human mother was a non-person. This would have unraveled many of the fundamental arguments and conclusions around which he (and many, many others) has built a career in secularized moral philosophy and bioethics. All he said was that it was "more difficult" to live out the principle than he thought before. Christians should know better than most how difficult it is to live out our own principles—and should therefore hesitate to claim that a particular moral vision is necessarily false if its adherents fail to live it out consistently.

That said, this story highlights two very important things that set up this chapter. First, there is no logical or consistent way for the current secularizing and even irreligious trajectory to be stopped short of denying fundamental equality for human beings with late-stage dementia. Second, Peter Singer is, perhaps, the best candidate imaginable for consistently living out a vision of the good, again, broadly shared among those who hold with a secularized vision of medicine and bioethics. While his inability to do so in this instance doesn't necessarily mean that this vision is false, it may be the kind of jolting story that can push a culture to begin thinking about hitting the pause button, catching our breath, and thinking hard about whether we want to keep hurrying down a cultural path on which more and more human beings are discarded as non-persons.

Late-Stage Dementia: Huge Problem Today, Disaster Tomorrow

It is difficult to face, not least because it portends the fate a good many of us will encounter as we age, but here are some sobering numbers about our contemporary moment from the Harvard NeuroDiscovery Center (HNC):[199]

- 5 million Americans have Alzheimer's disease

- 1 million have Parkinson's disease

- 400,000 have multiple sclerosis (MS)

- 30,000 have amyotrophic lateral sclerosis (ALS, or Lou Gehrig's disease)

The numbers are even more frightening when we consider the future, especially as people who make it to older ages tend to live longer and longer. If the rate of increase is the same over the next three decades, the HNC estimates that in the United States alone twelve million more people will have these neurodegenerative diseases. Worldwide, more than fifty million people are living with dementia and that number will double every twenty years.[200] There are about ten million new cases each year—one new case every three seconds. The disease affects a broad range of people but disproportionately affects otherwise-vulnerable populations, including Blacks.[201] The future problem is so clearly overwhelming that investors see in it an obvious money-making opportunity. MarketWatch.com has prepared a report (which costs over $4,000 for investors to access) whose landing page claims that because "the prevalence of neurodegenerative disorders is on the rise" there will be substantial "growth of the market over the forecast period."[202] A headline in *Fortune Business Insights* is even more direct: "Neurodegenerative Diseases Drugs Market to Worth USD 62.7 Billion by 2026."[203]

Because there is not much general recognition of the looming disaster, I reached out to those working in the field to understand the scope of the problem. Paula M. Taliaferro, MGS, LSW, a long-time consultant on aging and dementia issues, works with the Central Ohio Area Agency on Aging as an education and outreach specialist. She told me that "we are in no way prepared for the wave of people who are developing these conditions." While she has "seen great improvements in the conversations and in the options for families in [her] forty years as a clinician," the situation overall "is truly concerning."

A major concern is a shortage of caregivers and other workers, which Taliaferro said is already here "in a big way." That shortage is a great concern, but "the elephant in the room" is the additional shortage of those upon whom the caregivers depend: "nurse's aides, kitchen staff, housekeeping, and transportation drivers work for $9–$10 an hour with difficult working conditions, poor training, and long hours." She notes that these same people can make $15 an hour at Amazon or Walmart and also receive health benefits, so "it's not rocket science to understand the shortage." Going forward, Taliaferro argues that it will be an "enormous and probably defining issue in the next fifteen years" as we live longer lives and have fewer children to take care of us. "We are already in a panic, to be honest," she said. "The answer to this huge problem isn't super clear." The lack of an answer is especially stark given that finding a cure for such diseases continues to face major setbacks.[204]

Some see robots as the solution to this huge problem. While they "acknowledge the important role of human caregivers," the folks at Alzheimers.net (which, a few seconds after I had been on their website, sent me a pop-up asking if I wanted to chat with someone about home care) nevertheless insist that robots can keep a "watchful eye" on people with dementia and help combat feelings of isolation, thus taking pressure off human beings.[205] A WebMD article entitled "Robots May Soon Become Alzheimer's Caregivers" suggests that such machines can offer "a number of individualized applications that promote social connectivity."[206] An artificial intelligence expert recently received a prestigious award (bestowed annually to an entrepreneur who improves the lives of the elderly) for creating a toy seal intended to be the robotic companion of people with advanced dementia.[207] Given what I'm trying to show in this book, this is an interesting and telling development.

Though some people still argue that society needs to change in order to provide more human interaction for people with late-stage dementia,[208] many are inclined instead toward interactions with machines. We need to ask why. Below, I will discuss our response to the pandemic of neurological disease in more detail, but it is worth mentioning now that the United Kingdom has moved toward robots as a primary means of addressing the exacerbated loneliness among their nursing home population, about half of whom have some kind of dementia.[209]

High Cost, Low-Quality Care

Despite the shortage of adequately-paid and adequately-trained caregivers—leaving aside the explosion over the next two decades of people with dementia—the cost of treating and caring for those with dementia is extraordinary right here and right now. According to the *Journal of Alzheimer's Disease*, in the United States today 300 billion dollars is spent to care for those with dementia; globally the costs reach over 1 trillion dollars.[210] And hidden costs are often not factored into these calculations—like the anxiety or depression that family members develop in caring for a loved one with dementia, families that cut back on spending or dip into savings to support a loved one, or the costs they incur before a diagnosis is made.

According to the 2019 C.A.R.E. study from Northwestern Mutual Insurance—which includes all kinds of caregiving for elderly loved ones—"55% of caregivers are providing more than six hours a day of care over an expected average of almost 10 years of total care."[211] Over sixteen million people in the United States are unpaid caregivers for people with Alzheimer's disease.[212] In some cases, family and friends make a conscious choice to commit themselves to this caregiving time, but often it is a situation into which caregivers are thrust, largely without warning or adequate social support.[213]

The United Kingdom's Alzheimer's Society found that, even under their National Health Service, British citizens "are facing catastrophic costs" for the care and support of their loved ones.[214] And when the social safety net does provide the care they need, that care is of poor quality. Significantly, the Alzheimer's Society study also found that there is much better funding for the kinds and quality of care for other diseases (like cancer), which then require less sacrifice by loved ones. Harkening back to the previous chapter's discussion of NICE and QALYs, it is significant to note that the NHS at first refused to approve inexpensive drugs to treat Alzheimer's disease. Only public pressure caused them to relent and reverse course.[215]

In the United States, things aren't much better. Medicare, the government-run primary health insurance for most people over sixty-five, covers only inpatient hospital care and some prescription drugs for patients with dementia. If a physician determines that a patient is near death, it will also cover hospice care. But in cases where the person with dementia is not dying, it will pay for only one hundred days of nursing home care, and even then only in limited circumstances.[216] When we take into account the numbers listed above, this assistance is a drop in the bucket of the actual costs of treating and caring for someone with dementia. And with US fertility rates at historic lows, in future generations there will be far fewer children to care for their parents and grandparents.

Moreover, this is taking place when Medicare and other health-care costs are already adding significantly to the national budget deficit. The US government spends one trillion dollars, over a quarter of its budget, on health care. About three-fifths of this amount goes to Medicare.[217] The budget deficit for 2019 alone was about one trillion dollars, and in 2020 the national debt reached over *twenty-three trillion* dollars. Even without considering the massive increase in debt incurred from responding to the COVID-19 pandemic (estimates are that national debt will increase to thirty-three trillion by the end of the decade[218]), the federal government estimates that Medicare will be insolvent by 2026.[219] Major changes are being proposed, such as raising the age for Medicare eligibility from sixty-five to sixty-seven—which will require many older people to keep working, sometimes in ways that their bodies cannot reasonably handle.[220] As costs related to treating and caring for the growing numbers of people with dementia continue to rise dramatically, it is difficult not to see a financial disaster on the horizon—both for the government and for less-privileged US Americans who are trying to find a way to care for their loved ones.

It is also important to highlight just how bad—or even terrible—much of the care currently is. The 2019 World Alzheimer's Report focuses on neglect by medical caregivers as a major concern. Four in ten people believe that "doctors and nurses ignore people with dementia."[221] In chapter 3, we saw that one of the people Dr. Fins interviewed for *Rights Come to Mind* describes a clinic with a floor for "everybody who had no opportunity, or no prospect of ever being very alive. Alzheimer's patients, people who were in PVS. . . . If you went up there it was filthy, the staff was bad." When asked whether people with dementia were treated poorly, Paula Taliaferro responded, "Yes, yes, yes! They are often overmedicated and left to sit in a chair and wait for meals or showers." She also noted that those with money have better outcomes than those without, with the latter population "often warehoused in bad facilities that do little to meet any needs other than the most basic."

And far more often than we are prepared to admit, the care offered is not just inadequate: it is abusive. Studies by the University of California-Irvine's Center on Abuse and Neglect report abuse by about half of surveyed caregivers serving people with dementia.[222] The studies also note that about 60 percent of caregivers admit to verbally abusing those for whom they are providing care. The center notes that it is often difficult to find evidence of physical abuse, so loved ones should look for abrupt weight loss; bedrail or restraint injuries or bruises; unwashed hair, body, or clothes; fractures or concussions; and bedsores. Financial abuse, also a serious problem, is difficult to detect as well. The center recommends looking for missing cash, jewelry, or other valuables. Patients with late-stage dementia are susceptible not only to direct theft, but also to caregivers refusing to do certain things without "extra payment" or even trying to add themselves to a patient's will. Maddeningly, during the COVID-19 pandemic a number of US nursing homes stole their patients' $1,200 government stimulus checks.[223]

Already Less than Equal?

By now readers may have seen the connection between the situation of many so-called vegetative patients, such as those for whom Joseph Fins was advocating in chapter 3, and the situation of patients with late-stage dementia. Fins described how patients in the former group were "prone to depersonalization" and "almost relegated to the status of nonpersons." He based his observations mostly on two important facts: these so-called "vegetative" patients were segregated from the rest of the population, and they were not given the same diagnostic and prognostic care as patients with other diseases. People who have late-stage dementia are similarly segregated—sometimes even marginalized to the same floor of the clinic or hospital as "vegetative" patients. And health insurance (including government-provided insurance) treats dementia differently than it does other terminal illnesses.

To Fins's two important facts I would add both our slouch toward more robots instead of more personal interactions and our cultural willingness to put up with inadequate care and even abuse. And then we must carefully consider how the scarcity of health-care resources has compounded an already serious problem, an effect that will only grow more dramatic with time. Many of the social ingredients that led to denying the fundamental human equality of brain-dead human beings are now coalescing around the question of what to do in cases of late-stage dementia. Medicine and medical ethics are much further down the path toward secularization and even irreligion. The same central issue running throughout this book—whether human equality is fundamental or whether equality comes from having certain traits that not every human being has—presents itself here quite directly. Many human beings with late-stage dementia cannot be said to have rationality or self-awareness; the same was said, as we saw in previous chapters, of Terri Schiavo, Jahi McMath, and Alfie Evans. They are clearly living human beings, but as Singer so strongly insists, they no longer have the traits that make someone a person.

And though Singer is one of the few intellectuals to discuss his views on these matters publicly, he is not alone in his moral reasoning and his conclusion. Dan W. Brock, a philosopher at Brown University, argues quite directly that "destruction of personal identity from severe dementia" means that human beings in this situation have no claim to life-sustaining health care.[224] To be sure, some thinkers have pushed back against the positions of Brock and Singer.[225] But for decades there has been a genuine debate in academic literature about whether human beings with late-stage dementia matter the same as other human beings.[226]

And in some ways, in some places, there is already evidence that denying the humanity of people with late-stage dementia has become more than just an academic point of view and has made its way into areas of medical practice. For instance, recently in the Netherlands (a country which has a longstanding practice of euthanasia and assisted suicide) a doctor who euthanized a patient with dementia against the patient's will was found not guilty of murder.[227] The patient had previously requested physician-assisted suicide, but later (after she developed dementia) said at three different times that she had changed her mind and no longer wanted to die. The doctor and the patient's husband dismissed her views, conspired to have a deadly drug put in her coffee, and stealthily killed her. After acquitting the doctor, the Netherlands formally moved to legalize sedating patients with dementia before killing them—in part because, the new code claims, "it is not necessary for the doctor to agree with the patient the time and manner in which euthanasia will be given."[228] Readers in the United States who assume that such things could never happen here should not feel superior to the Dutch. The State of California (which only recently legalized assisted suicide) is already feeling serious pressure to euthanize patients with Alzheimer's disease.[229] Once we are on the slope of legalized medical killing, it is very difficult to stop the slide. And though we haven't quite reached the level of the Dutch when it comes to direct killing, nursing homes are already overmedicating people with dementia (often with antipsychotic drugs) simply to keep them "docile" and generally in need of less care.[230]

Dementia and the Pandemic

When I first started writing this book in 2018, I envisioned a chapter on dementia as a prediction. But as I got into the research, and especially when the COVID-19 pandemic hit, this chapter began to stand between prediction and description. In my previous book, *Resisting Throwaway*

Culture (2019), I noted that people with dementia are a throwaway population in our culture, but didn't cite any stories of someone literally being discarded. During the pandemic, however, we learned that nursing homes across the country kicked out residents with dementia to make room for COVID-positive residents who would make them more money. One of those residents, eighty-eight-year-old RC Kendrick, was found wandering the streets of Los Angeles less than twenty-four hours after being dumped into an unregulated boardinghouse.[231]

During the pandemic, people with dementia have been one of the most at-risk populations. Evidence showing that having dementia seems to increase the risk for serious complications and death from COVID-19[232] led the CDC to add dementia to the list of conditions that place individuals at more risk.[233] But beyond the connection between dementia and physical vulnerability to COVID-19 lies another concern: ableism in health-care providers. It would be strange indeed if the pandemic were somehow immune from the discrimination toward the disabled in health care that we've seen throughout this book.

During my research, I learned a lot from a certified nursing assistant (I'll call her "Annella") who started working on the dementia floor of a US nursing home around the beginning of the pandemic. When I asked her about the population she worked with, she noted how sad and angry she was about the unequal treatment they received. "No one I've seen here gets palliative care or hospice," Annella said. "They all simply get dehydrated to death. We're told in our training that it is a good thing." In her experience, most doctors stayed away from her facility and let an understaffed, underpaid nursing and nursing assistant crew (often without the necessary personal protective equipment) care for patients with unimaginable needs. Many of the patients under her care desperately needed a podiatrist, but lack of proper care left them with mangled, misshapen feet and toes. They developed deadly pressure injuries due to lack of turning. They sat for hours with soiled clothes. Sometimes they weren't even fed.

The results of this neglect have been heartbreaking—and deadly. An AP investigation found that for every two nursing home residents who died of COVID-19 during the pandemic, another died of "other causes"—including tens of thousands who died of isolation and neglect.[234] Another investigation found that deaths of people with dementia rose more than 20 percent above normal in summer 2020. During this time there were eleven thousand "excess deaths" of people with dementia—a number *Politico* described as "staggering" and attributed, among other things, to "lapses in nursing home care."[235] Robert Anderson, chief of mortality statistics at the CDC, said of these numbers: "There's something wrong, there's something going on and it needs to be sorted out. This is highly unusual." Indeed. Sometimes what's "going on" is criminal behavior. In September 2020 the *New York Times* reported on the medical director of a Massachusetts veterans' home being charged with criminal neglect for deciding to combine healthy and infected residents from two dementia wards into one. One employee of the facility called it "the most insane thing I ever saw in my entire life."[236]

Part of what is almost certainly going on in these cases is something that has been highlighted throughout this book: a concern about limited resources. Consistent with what we've seen thus far, when difficult decisions about resources have to be made, the populations considered to be less than equal on the basis of their disability are marginalized. Fortunately, during the pandemic disability rights groups have insisted on calling out such practices. In one particularly dramatic case, in the *Los Angeles Times* they blasted Governor Gavin Newsom of California for approving a discriminatory protocol for health-care rationing which, they noted ominously, "communicates what the medical establishment and state government think about disabled people and older adults."[237] These discriminatory practices had already been baked into the emergency rationing plans of several other states as well. Alabama's, for instance, deemed persons with "moderate to severe dementia" to be "unlikely candidates for ventilator support" in case of a shortage.[238] In this case, after a complaint was filed, the Office of Civil Rights at the Department of Health and Human Services forced the State of Alabama to change its policy.[239] One of the few silver linings of the pandemic, in my view, is that a light has been shined on terrible things that otherwise would have remained hidden in the darkness.

Beyond Dementia

Claiming that trait X is required for fundamental equality or that loss of trait Y means a loss of fundamental equality opens the door for powerful ableist forces to determine who is in and who is out, to determine which lives are part of a community of equals and which are outside that community. To use the language of the United Kingdom's NHS, disability rights activists call out those who argue that some individuals no longer "benefit from their lives," as well as the basis on which they make such a judgment. Generally speaking, it is privileged, able-bodied people who make these calls. And often, again, directly or indirectly, they decide who is in and who is out on the basis of allocating scarce resources. In addition to being true, fundamental human equality serves as a bulwark against such arbitrary impositions of a particular vision of the good onto disabled populations.

And there is no reason in principle that a secularizing and irreligious trajectory will stop at human populations who are so neurologically devastated that they are no longer aware of themselves. Recall key actualized traits many thinkers highlight as necessary for a human being to share in the fundamental equality of persons: rationality, autonomy, productivity, volition, communication, and the like. Then consider the following case study and ask yourself: What is to stop powerful people with a vision of personhood focused on such traits from arguing that the lives of human beings like Amelia's are no longer beneficial to them?

Amelia Rivera was born with a genetic disorder called Wolf-Hirschhorn Syndrome.[240] She had uncharacteristic facial features, delayed growth, and significant intellectual disability. Human beings with her condition rarely speak and have a significantly limited ability to comprehend or understand.[241] Her parents loved her unconditionally, however, and were willing to do whatever they could to help her—including getting her a new kidney when it became clear that she would need one. To that end, they consulted with the prestigious Children's Hospital of Philadelphia. To their shock, they were told Amelia was not a transplant candidate because of her "mental retardation."

Her parents refused to accept the medical team's decision and took the case public. Only under extreme negative pressure did the hospital relent, agree to the transplant, and issue a public statement: "We appreciate the role the Riveras have played in helping us recognize opportunities for improvement and believe we are a better institution as a result." But, Amelia's mother said, in the months after their story became public "a lot of people have reached out to us personally to share similar stories, to tell us heartbreaking stories of how their loved ones were denied simple medical care, dental care, eyeglasses—because medical professionals felt that this person's quality of life wasn't good enough to get this care." After her daughter received the donor kidney and was clearly thriving, Chrissy Rivera became an important public voice on questions of disability and medicine. Speaking at a dinner hosted by the Special Olympics, she poignantly put her finger on a central problem this book highlights: "I don't have a concrete solution to change the stigma that exists in the medical community."

During the pandemic, I wrote and spoke a number of times about the case of Michael Hickson, a middle-aged disabled Black man who was infected with COVID-19 while in a nursing home and who later died in an Austin,

Texas, hospital.[242] But he didn't die of COVID-19 alone—his wife Melissa described his death as murder. The medical team decided not to treat or feed him for six days, after which he died. A (legal) recording of her conversation with Michael's doctor reveals the ableist reasoning behind his death. Although she and the doctor both agreed that Michael should not be intubated, the recording begins with Melissa still wanting Michael to be treated aggressively. His doctor, however, claimed that aggressive treatment wouldn't "help him improve" and said, "right now, his quality of life . . . he doesn't have much of one."

Melissa responded, "What do you mean? Because he's paralyzed with a brain injury, he doesn't have quality of life?" Michael's doctor, the one charged with his most intimate and important physical care, simply said, "Correct." Melissa got the doctor to admit that patients in Michael's situation have survived before. But he noted ominously that her husband's case "doesn't fit those." Michael's "quality of life is different from theirs," his doctor explained. The three of his patients who survived in this kind of situation "were walking and talking people." Melissa tried to make the case that her husband has value despite his disability, but the doctor had had enough and said, "I don't mean to be frank or abrasive, but at this point, we are going to do what we feel is best for him, along with the state, and this is what we decided." Game over. The medical team decided that people who don't walk and talk like the rest of us don't count the same.

Just a few months later an investigative report from National Public Radio found another, eerily similar example

of deadly medical ableism.[243] In April of 2020 a vibrant—
and severely disabled—woman named Sarah McSweeny
suddenly fell ill with a strange (non-COVID) pneumonia.
As her pneumonia worsened it became clear that she would
need to go on a ventilator. According to Kimberly Conger,
the nurse manager of Sarah's group home, this was necessary to let the antibiotics work and for the aspirated lung to
rest and heal. But then something shocking happened: the
physician in charge of her care said he wanted an order that
Sarah should not be resuscitated or intubated. Though she
was "full code" (Sarah wanted everything done to save her
life), her physician said it was "a matter of risk vs. quality
of life." When Sarah's home nurse and guardian pointed
out that she did have quality of life—among other things,
Sarah absolutely loved country music—her physician said,
"Oh, she can walk? And talk?" After several atypical decisions (including choosing not to feed her through an IV
rather than a g-tube that was giving her problems) Sarah
died of sepsis due to aspirational pneumonia.

These and many other examples of profound disability
may lead those with such ableist beliefs to the conclusion
that there are even more categories of human beings who
don't count the same as others. (Indeed, NPR has uncovered
significant evidence that, during the pandemic, hospitals
pressured patients with intellectual disabilities to sign do-
not-resuscitate orders before being admitted.[244]) Physicians
and medical ethicists who operate from a secularized and
even irreligious perspective have significant power, and
tend to focus on traits like rationality, autonomy, communication, and volitional choice. Given what we have seen
thus far in this book, we now find ourselves at a terrible

place in which we must ask if even more moderately-disabled populations will also be seen as less than equal when compared to the able-bodied and able-minded. And then we must ask what might happen to them, especially in a health-care system under intense resource pressure.

Time to Speak Up

In several ways, we now find ourselves in a place like the one we were in just before the Harvard brain death committee's report. The intellectual and moral foundations supporting the fundamental equality of a vulnerable population of human beings are being undermined, especially by secularizing and irreligious currents in medicine and medical ethics. And on the horizon there is a dramatic and even horrific scarcity of health-care resources—a scarcity which, if history is any guide, may lead over time to the broadly held view that human beings with late-stage dementia have had "their personal identity destroyed" by their disease and thus are not owed life-sustaining treatment or care. So while in a way these profoundly disabled human beings are already being treated as "less than" or "other" compared to able-minded human beings, the worst may be yet to come. Recall Dr. Beecher's striking claim that a failure to accept a neurological definition of death meant that "the curable, the salvageable, can thus be sacrificed to the hopelessly damaged and unconscious who consume the time and space and money better devoted to those who could be helped."[245] There is little to prevent Beecher's claim reaching well beyond brain death to human beings with late-stage dementia—and perhaps further.

Conclusion

The desperation surrounding the gradual loss of one's mental faculties, and a media sympathetic to a secularizing and irreligious understanding of personal (rather than human) equality, has led to changes in the broader culture well beyond the academic and medical communities. While writing this book, I came across a *New York Times* feature story about Alma Shaver, a wife and mother who was sliding into the later stages of dementia.[246] She knew her name, but not her age. She forgot the faces of her children and how to sew. As things, got worse, Alma began to slip "beyond a murky fog that her husband could not join." According to the story, her husband's response was to shoot his wife in her sleep and then shoot himself. The reporter did not describe this action as a horrific murder-suicide, nor as a terrible example of domestic violence built on ableism and male aggression. On the contrary, the author went out of her way to paint Alma's husband as a sympathetic figure, strongly implying that the killing was justified. The story left no doubt that it is understandable, perhaps reasonable, that Alma's husband killed her.

Though it does say something significant about our cultural trajectory that the *New York Times* would print a story which sends such a message about the value of those with late-stage dementia, for the moment this seems to be a minority position. The much more common reaction is simply to ignore the realities on which this chapter focuses. When I asked Wendy Perry, acting head of learning and development at the Dementia Services Centre at the University of Stirling in Scotland, about my research for this chapter, she made a simple yet profound point: "That a process exists which strips away at the core of one's personality, leaving the individual at the mercy of others who may or may not subscribe to upholding and reinforcing their uniqueness, is terrifying to consider. . . . I can quickly shut a conversation down simply by telling people what I do for a living. Most often it is easier to not recognize that that stage of the disease process even exists."

But we can no longer be silent. If the sobering numbers documented at the beginning of this chapter are any indication, many of us will face this disease. Many more of us have already faced it, are facing it now, or will face it in the future, with a loved one. If the hundreds of messages I've received in reaction to my media appearances on this issue during the pandemic provide any guide, there is already a profound level of pain and anger surrounding issues of dementia care in the United States. Doing nothing either lets the problem fester or gives ground to those who will solve the problem by marginalizing and even discarding as human non-persons those with late-stage dementia and other disabilities. At this point neither option is acceptable. It is time to stand up, be heard, and sound the alarm. We have put ourselves on a cultural trajectory which leads naturally and logically to claiming that millions of human beings with a profound intellectual disability do not have fundamental equality with the rest of us.

In the next and final chapter of this book, I offer some thoughts about how we might reverse our cultural course.

Chapter Seven

Reversing Course

I wrote this book to tell a story of a powerful and deeply disturbing cultural trajectory and sound the alarm. But in this final chapter I want to propose what can be done to reverse course. If we do nothing, we face the prospect that fundamental human equality may die out as a cultural concept, placing millions of human beings with late-stage dementia, and many other vulnerable disabled populations, at serious risk.

In what follows I suggest short-term and medium-term strategies for turning the cultural tide. In the short term (say, immediately to about two years from now) I suggest strategies that individuals and communities can implement without relying on those who do not share their vision of the good about fundamental human equality. In the medium term (about two years to about ten years from now) I focus on what it may take to create an effective cultural antidote to the poison of secularizing irreligion. This requires engaged dialogues between those with different visions of the good, especially in the medical and medical ethics communities, with the hope of finding unity around the principle of fundamental human equality. In case we come to the longer term (about ten to twenty years from now) without having begun to move in a different direction, God forbid, the conclusion to this book offers some ideas about how religious institutions will need to mobilize *en masse* to meet what can only be described as a cultural disaster.

But let's start by thinking positive. In the short and medium term, what can we do to avoid this fate?

Short Term: Living Out a Culture of Responsibility, Encounter, and Hospitality

The first thing that we can and should do—right now, immediately—is to sound the cultural alarm. For the moment, the idea of the profoundly disabled losing their equal human dignity at the end of their lives still shocks most people enough to take notice and ask themselves with some urgency what led us to this point. Many may have personal experience with dementia in their own social circles and, in their more courageous and authentic moments, are concerned that they may face it in their own future. The numbers laid out in the previous chapter speak for themselves; and enough people are familiar with stories like those of Jahi, Terri, or Alfie and can connect their own experience with these patients'.

But in addition to sounding the alarm, those of us who share the concern can take steps almost immediately (and certainly in the short-term) to live our lives as signs of opposition to a throwaway culture which discards or otherwise marginalizes human non-persons as having lost their fundamental dignity. To start, as individuals and families we can live out a counterculture of responsibility, encounter, and hospitality. Here are just a few ideas:

- Put our families first. Realize that just as our parents and other adults in our family circles had an obligation to make great sacrifices for us, we have an obligation to make great sacrifices for them.

- Make choices about housing, debt, and living situations that allow us to care for our parents or other older family members (although due to varying levels of economic privilege, not everyone will be able to do so). So many otherwise-privileged people become "house poor" or "debt poor"—often (but not always) driven by cultural consumerism—and get caught in a two-income trap that handcuffs them to jobs and/or places which keep them from attending to the needs of older family members.

- Resist the cultural temptation—often (but not always) driven by cultural consumerism—to live far away from family members who would support us, or to live far from those we have a familial obligation to support in the first place. It is worth noting that larger families are easier to manage if they live close to extended family.

- Resist the cultural temptation—again, often (but not always) driven by cultural consumerism—to limit artificially the number of children we bear, adopt, or foster. Smaller families face more challenges in supporting one another than larger ones do. Especially given the "longer-term" recommendations we will see in the conclusion, it is worth noting that larger families also tend to produce more religious vocations.

- Resist the cultural temptation—once again, often (but not always) driven by cultural consumerism—to think of the home as closed to all but a single nuclear family. We can work to create spaces for older family members, especially as they lose the capacities which a secularized and irreligious culture decides once made their lives a benefit to them.

- Refuse to have family members cared for by robots when other options are available. Once normalized, the Trojan horse of computer caregivers will fundamentally change our relationship to these (and other) vulnerable populations.

- Regularly and formally volunteer in nursing homes, especially those that serve people with dementia, not only to signal publicly the equal human dignity of these populations, but also to aid overworked caregivers and staff.

- Invite someone who isn't as plugged into these issues to accompany you on your volunteer visits and encourage encounters between younger and older generations. The power of encounter is formidable. Recall from chapter 2 journalist Rachel Aviv's visit with Jahi McMath and her family. Simply being in the same space convinced her of Jahi's fundamental human equality, and through her *New Yorker* article that countercultural view was engaged by tens of thousands.

- Consider (second?) careers or intense service projects oriented toward human beings who have lost or are losing the traits our dominant culture finds valuable. Many people find themselves trapped (again, often because of consumerism) in careers and projects they dislike, or even hate. Getting out of those careers may free us up to meet the deep challenges ahead.

- Work to ensure government and other resources to empower families to take care of their elderly and disabled loved ones at home. This is an important goal on multiple levels, but it is also quite cost-effective relative to care in nursing homes.[247]

- Work to ensure government and other resources to provide significantly better care in nursing homes (including better pay and reimbursement rates), especially for specialized dementia care in day-care centers or via in-home and community-based care. I've argued elsewhere that this is a brilliant opportunity for the pro-life movement to work with social justice activists in supporting policies that defend the vulnerable and prioritize the (extended) family.[248]

Notice how in the above recommendations consumerism often appears as a force to be resisted. As mentioned in chapter 2, in a post-Christian culture like ours the dominant views of personhood have been linked closely with notions about productivity, ability, and consumerism. We would do well, therefore, to live our lives as signs of contradiction in a culture whose idol is buying and selling and to resist the idea that your value comes from the things you can consume or create.

Broader communities, especially religious communities, can also be signs of opposition to the culture. Both Jeff Bishop in *The Anticipatory Corpse*[249] and Brian Volck in his review of that same book[250] suggest that local religious communities (churches, synagogues, and mosques, in particular) have the capacity to resist the secularizing and irreligious forces being brought to bear upon contemporary medicine and medical ethics. Bishop, for instance, says that religious communities' practices of care and communal interdependence may be a source for renewal in a culture that currently tends to be shaped by a different vision. Volck warns that, while this is true, too many religious communities have been weakened by the very vision that must be resisted—he sees in particular a "culturally accommodated Christianity" made up of supposedly autonomous, atomized individual persons rather than genuinely connected communities. But Volck also notes that creating places where fundamental human equality is recognized, defended, and supported in community is something religious institutions have always done, and should be doing now. In my own work, I've often pointed out how many people (especially young people) yearn for the kind of belonging that comes from living in such interdependent communities. It is time to get to work, especially for Christian churches.

And we have some good examples to choose from as our models. Recalling the Middle Ages can be particularly instructive. Elaine Stratton Hild describes a moment concerning physical illness and religious practice in the life of a typical fourteenth-century Augustinian monastery:[251]

The leader of the community, the prior, came to the brother's sickbed to hear his confession. The others gathered and processed to the infirmary with oil for anointing, incense, the communion host, a cross, and candles. They assembled in the room, singing antiphons and psalms as their sick brother was anointed. The gathered brothers sang songs of petition, using words from the Gospels: "Lord, come down to heal my son before he dies," and songs of hope: "Jesus said to him, Go, your son lives." After the anointing, the brothers arranged a schedule so that at least one person remained always at his bedside. Prayers were said for him at the daily public Mass.

During the late Middle Ages this basic approach, says Hild, was not limited to monasteries, but was broadly shared across Western Europe. One of several common practices involved the "integral role" of the community, which provided physical care and also offered spiritual support via presence, prayers, chants, and songs. "Sickness and death," she emphasizes, "were not individual experiences." Even in our contemporary context we can find similar monastic examples of how to create a community around the sick and dying. Nicolas Diat's new book *A Time to Die: Monks on the Threshold of Eternal Life* describes particularly interesting and countercultural practices.[252] Another modern-day example worth citing is the hospice volunteer program initiated in the Louisiana State Penitentiary, as featured in the documentary *Serving Life*.[253]

We can also look to several lay religious communities that provide similarly moving examples. I'm particularly close to the Focolare Movement—a lay Catholic group with deep dialogical ties to Protestant Christians, religious non-Christians, and secular conversation partners. In many situations I have witnessed first-hand the power of the "spirituality of unity" that informs their life. It is particularly powerful for those in their circles who are facing struggles with late-stage dementia. Indeed, their focus on a unified community of love is directed not just at the individuals who are bearing the disease, but also the family caring for them.

The Focolare's monthly magazine *Living City* published the moving details of the experience a friend of the Movement had in caring for her husband.[254] At one point she describes being incredibly frightened because her husband was hallucinating all night, she had no medication to give him, and none of the formal caregivers upon whom they normally relied were available. She shared her feelings of hopelessness, anger, and a near-inability to cope with the situation. But a few weeks after this moment, a meeting with members of the Focolare changed everything for her. When they asked her how things were going, at first she kept her feelings internalized; but their persistent attempts, thoughtful and careful, to reach out to her in love nudged her to share, through sobbing and tears, the full reality of her situation. The support from these friends reminded her that she also had God's support and that she must turn to one of the most important resources available to her: prayer. With the support of the Focolare community, and by placing the situation in God's hands, she said, "everything was put into perspective" and the care of her husband "was no longer a burden."

As my last bullet point above suggests, we need to better fund nursing homes so that they can hire more health-care providers who have the time and incentives to respect the dignity of their patients. This is not about class, but about realism in the current marketplace. Recall the emphasis Paula Taliaferro put on the struggle some folks have to meet their monthly bills, forcing them to choose between meaningful work as a nursing aide for $9 per hour, or working at Walmart for $15 per hour. We must be willing to pay competitive wages so as to attract compassionate workers like Annella (mentioned in the previous chapter) who are willing to treat patients with dementia like human beings. Consider this moving example of how she showed respect for the fundamental human equality of a patient:

> I think "Rebecca" was one of my favorites. The first time I met her, she was on the fourth, rehab, just had come back from the hospital, and the fourth floor was packed. Everyone was coming in from the hospital, and everyone was on droplet precautions so that meant we had to gown and mask up before even entering their rooms—only there weren't enough gowns and we only had one mask for a week. Lights were going off constantly and there was only one other CNA with me. We did nothing but run all night.

The rehab floor isn't for residents. There's nothing homey about it, it's more like a hotel, except with ports for tubes coming out of the walls, and hospital beds and bathrooms. It's one long hallway, and Rebecca was in the second to last room.

She had been a local photographer, a professional, and she was beautiful. You could tell that she used to carry herself gracefully. But when I met her, she was in a hospital gown with an IV attached to her and she had soaked through the diaper, her pressure injury wound pad was saturated along with the bed, and she was crying.

I don't know how long she'd been left there by herself, but it had been a long time. The look on her face was of lost hope.

I think that was the first time I got really angry at the injustice of all of it.

Changing patients is like a choreographed dance. You gather your supplies, you put the bed up high, and you do everything in halves— you strip half of the bed, roll them away from you, tuck everything tight under them, roll them back to you, and the same with the diapers. Roll, roll, roll. It takes so much out of them, when they have so little energy to spare that it's exhausting. But I got her cleaned up, dry, we washed her face, put cream on her arms and legs, got fresh sheets on, and I got her covered up with fresh sheets and a blanket. Pretty soon Rebecca was as snug as a bug in a rug, fast asleep with a very different look on her face.

Such an experience nearly moved me to tears—it seemed like such a dramatic and unusual example of loving someone. But Annella is right in insisting that we shouldn't consider what she did to be a big deal. We shouldn't be moved merely because our elders are treated with the basic respect due to all human beings. But we often are. The mere fact that someone can be so moved by her example demonstrates our need to be evangelical in our attempts to change our eldercare culture.

It is one thing to be salt and light for a culture through, as Volck describes them, practices and liturgies that honor the commonly understood dignity of human beings. But it is clear that even if these practices and liturgies become publicly influential—and even evangelical—we will still need intentional strategies for dialogue (another gift of Focolare members, from whom I have learned much) by which we can develop a suitable antidote to the poison that threatens fundamental human equality.

Medium Term: Building Bridges of Dialogue

Effective dialogues do not start from the naïve sense that anyone can convince another person of something. On the contrary, effective dialogues acknowledge up front the fundamental differences which may exist. For the dialogues I'm proposing here, we should be clear that even Christians disagree about the central idea undergirding our equal dignity: what it means to be made in the image of God. The Abrahamic religions—"people of the book," meaning Muslims, Christians, and Jews—have even more substantial disagreements about this matter. And believers in different kinds of divine reality, along with believers in no divine reality at all, presumably may reject altogether the idea that human beings are made in the image of God.

But by acknowledging these differences—from the small to the very large—we can focus on where we can find significant agreement. Most traditional Christians, Muslims, and Jews agree that all human beings have inherent and equal dignity because of a shared nature that reflects the image and likeness of God. Recall, for instance, in chapter 2 the religious exemptions regarding brain death carved out largely by Orthodox Jews in New Jersey and New York, and in chapter 5 the Muslim fatwa regarding little Tafida's moral standing.

Those outside of these traditions might disagree with the theological ideas, but—if they do not have (or can at least put aside) secularizing or irreligious approaches—perhaps a genuine dialogue can find an overlapping consensus that allows them to support the conclusion. Here it is worth highlighting that more and more "Christian atheists" or "religious agnostics" say they do not believe in a god or gods; nevertheless, they uphold something akin to religious moral beliefs and often still identify in some ways as "culturally" Catholic, Jewish, or Muslim. This phenomenon ranges across the political spectrum: from Douglas

Murray, who identifies with the political right, to Dan Savage, who identifies with the political left, and lots of folks who fall into neither category. If the arguments and evidence presented in this book are considered dispassionately and fairly, isn't it reasonable that those who hold with no particular system of faith might reach the same moral conclusions that Christians, Muslims, and Jews do? Even if they cannot accept the way we got there?

Some may consider this a foolish hope, especially because—as I have demonstrated—some who have power are explicitly hostile to religious points of view. But we've seen that minds and hearts do change about these matters. From the experiences of Rachel Aviv, Joseph Fins, and Justice MacDonald, we know positions on these matters are not static. Even those whose history or public profile puts them among the most unlikely converts do in fact change their positions. The lead singer of the Sex Pistols, Johnny Rotten, a former punk rocker, has become a public advocate for those with dementia.[255] Buoyed by the hope that these changes can be replicated, what tools of dialogue do we have?

The first, I suggest, is a series of general values that we largely share. Most of those who operate from a secularized and irreligious perspective may not follow a general commitment to fundamental equality consistently, but they do have one. Such a commitment often makes them suspicious of consumerism and the measuring of value based on levels of burden or productivity. They recognize, at least in a general way, the injustice of ableism and in other contexts they support the disability rights communities.

Many are also generally suspicious of claims to individual autonomy, especially when made by those who have power over vulnerable populations. Those with a commitment to fundamental and social justice, including large numbers of individuals who are comfortable with secularized values and who do not share religious motives, agree that there cannot be a "contextual" basis for moral, legal, and social value. Justice demands that we treat the vulnerable as the equals of the powerful at all times, even when this is deeply inconvenient (like when doing so strains our resources), and perhaps *especially* when it is deeply inconvenient. The objectively true fact that the vulnerable have fundamental equality with those who are not vulnerable cannot change simply because social context changes.

It is significant that in our racial justice moment, our post-George Floyd world, we are laser-focused on the *objective value* of human beings, a value that those who think differently must accept whether they like it or not. There is no room for squishy moral relativism here. Indeed, it is striking to see how the fundamental value during this racial justice moment is also the fundamental value at the heart of this book. For example, one of the success stories in police reform relative to its relationship to the Black community took place in Camden, New Jersey. Among other things, Camden dramatically changed how their officers are trained to focus on diffusing encounters and to intervene if they see colleagues mistreating people. According to the *New York Times*, "Police officials talk about the 'sanctity of life' as the overarching thread connecting many of the changes."[256] This is confirmed by a report from the Police

Executive Research Forum (PERF), which challenges conventional thinking on police use of force.[257] The first line of the report reads: "Ultimately, this report is about the sanctity of all human life."

With these tools and concepts in common, we can engage in a fruitful, genuine dialogue about whether and how social context—like scarce health-care resources—may be putting at risk the equality of vulnerable populations. Of particular interest will be exchanges about whether and how a sense that someone is a "burden" or "unproductive" seeps into cultural attitudes about their moral status and value. Shared general values can foster important discussions about how placing undue emphasis on capacities like autonomy, self-awareness, consciousness, or communication reinforces an ableist culture that values particular abilities and undermines the equal moral and legal standing of disabled human beings who may not have those abilities in an actualized state.

These points by themselves would sustain a hopeful dialogue, but even more common ground can be highlighted. Those who operate from a secularized perspective may conclude that focusing on actualized traits like rationality and autonomy may be ableist and ought to be rejected, but nevertheless reject the idea that the lives of human beings (as the kinds of living creatures they are) matter *because* they are created in the image and likeness of God. But even without a theological basis, might it be possible to cultivate dialogue or even find overlapping consensus regarding the equal moral value of all human creatures, regardless of age, level of ability, disease, injury, etc.?

I think so. As discussed in chapter 3, some significant thinkers are starting to consider human consciousness as a product of the human animal in a holistic way, rather than as a mere product of the brain. A full exposition of this argument goes beyond the scope of this particular discussion, but other secular thinkers have held similar views of the human person. Aristotle didn't think of the spiritual aspect of human beings—their soul—in a dualistic way, where the soul could somehow depart a living human body. In fact, he strongly disagreed with the dualistic view of his mentor, Plato, who thought of the soul as a ghost or spirit inside a shell or machine. Aristotle instead thought of the soul as the form of the body or the actuality of a living body. For Aristotle, a living body and its soul or essence are no more separable than the impression made by a metal seal can be separated from the wax onto which it has been pressed. In this view, the particular nature or essence of human beings comes not from gaining certain traits that they can express, but from having a particular nature that they attain as a prenatal child.

As a pagan philosopher not motivated by the Bible's claim that human beings are made in the image and likeness of God, Aristotle and his followers (both then and now) demonstrate that it is not necessary to accept the theological claims at the heart of this book in order to dialogue about the common nature of human beings and the source of their fundamental equality. So yes, some may reject the idea that human beings are made in the image and likeness of God. But at the same time, without too much trouble, we can imagine a secular disability rights activist who rejects a traits-centered approach to person-hood and instead adopts an Aristotelian (or similar) approach.[258] Such a philosophical approach throws open doors to significant and productive dialogue between those who operate from secularized and irreligious principles and those who operate from religious beliefs concerning the fundamental human equality of all human creatures.

Such dialogue also reveals that there cannot be an ideologically neutral view from nowhere about what grounds belief in fundamental equality. Time and time again this book has demonstrated how discussion can focus upon first principles, chief loves, transcendental values, visions of the good, and ultimate concerns. But no one—whether a secular Aristotelian, a Catholic Thomist, a Muslim human rights activist, a Jewish casuist, an irreligious utilitarian, a care feminist, or someone with any other perspective—can claim not to begin from a place of foundational, committed ideology. A genuine dialogue that recognizes this fact cannot welcome only certain ideologies and exclude those that are deemed undesirable. Those who approach the questions raised in this book from an explicitly religious vision of the good don't expect or need special treatment. But they do need to be treated the same as others who base their fundamental values and ideas on a secularized vision of the good. An authentic dialogue in which participants are on an even playing field can serve as a powerful antidote to the poison of singling out religious traditions for hostility. This kind of dialogue could take place in many different contexts: the halls of Congress, long-form podcasts, college seminar tables, Thanksgiving dinners, and yes, even in the discipline of bioethics.[259]

What I am proposing may seem unreasonably optimistic. I'm under no illusions: this proposed dialogue may not in practice be productive and may not bring about significant changes in our cultural trajectory. In a moment I will conclude the book by focusing on "longer-term" suggestions for how, if dialogue is not productive, traditional Christians and other religious believers may respond. But before we get there it might be helpful to reflect on what those who want to uphold fundamental human equality might have to learn from our partners in this dialogue. First, we can learn, as Jeff Bishop suggests, to mourn the tragedy of the situations presented in this book.[260] While it is especially important to uphold the moral, legal, and social equality of the most profoundly disabled human beings, it also is important that the lives of human beings like Jahi, Terri, Alfie, and those with late-stage dementia not be used as ammunition in a culture war. The lives that their families envisioned for and with them became impossible, and this ought to be mourned. It is right to defend and celebrate the intrinsic and equal value of the life that remains. But it may be that dialogue with those who think differently can remind us that it is possible to uphold fundamental human equality while at the same time acknowledging that something important has been lost, tragically lost, and it is appropriate to mourn such a loss. It may indeed be the case that in some tragic situations, life-sustaining treatment (not basic human concern and care) can be ethically withdrawn. Fundamental human equality cannot be honored if such withdrawal is done with the intention of aiming at their death because, for instance, their life is supposedly no longer a benefit to them. But if it is done in a situation where death is foreseen, not intended, and for a proportionately serious reason (say, when the treatment is overly burdensome), such a removal may reflect the tragic nature of the loss that has taken place.

How can health-care providers be engaged in this kind of dialogue? We saw in chapter 1 just how deeply secularizing and irreligious forces have shaped the culture of medicine and the difficult challenge this presents. But so much of the damage done to fundamental human equality in the broader culture began within the field of medicine and is currently sustained by the structures that sustain medicine itself, making it difficult to imagine how we could reverse course as a culture without reversing course in the way medicine is envisioned and put into practice. Dare we hope things could change?

Recall the views of Tracy and Michael Balboni, the physician-theologian team at Harvard Medical School from chapter 1. They suggest we need to reform health-care culture—in which the explicit focus is on imminent questions, setting aside the metaphysical, the transcendent, and the ultimate. What this creates, they argue, are medical structures "where it is increasingly difficult for patients to receive spiritual care from within their own spiritual traditions."[261] This works against the fullness of the good of a hospital's or clinic's patients—who, the data show, would prefer to receive care based on a vision of the good from their own tradition. The Balbonis' approach leads to less patient-physician conflict, less unneeded and costly care, and greater use of hospice, as well as other intangible improvements. To move in this direction, of course, health-care institutions would need to stop proceeding as if their current approach is neutral, rather than driven by their own tradition-dependent vision of the good. They should instead avoid "spiritual coercion" and forthrightly offer approaches to care that reflect the pluralism and diversity of their patients.

The Balbonis are well aware that this cannot happen immediately, which is why I've located this goal in medium-term range—two to ten years from now. The habits of thinking are too ingrained for such a transformation to take deep hold in the field of medicine in the next couple years. The Balbonis want to pursue a "gradual unfolding" through "scientific testing, trial, and public evaluation toward the common good." Done correctly, it could lead to a genuine dialogue about first principles, chief loves, transcendental values, visions of the good, and ultimate concerns, in which secularized and irreligious hostility would have no home.

How likely is this to happen, even in the medium term? Again, given what we saw in chapter 1, it looks like a significant challenge. But important seeds have been planted which give cause for significant hope. The fact that the Professors Balboni are welcomed and cherished members of the Harvard Medical School community is a hopeful sign all by itself. The fact that Harvard medical students take courses with them suggests that the dialogue has already begun. And exciting things are happening in other places as well.

For instance, at the medical school at St. Louis University (a Catholic, Jesuit institution), a joint MD/

PhD program in health-care ethics trains future physicians in bioethics that take religious ideas seriously. Students can take courses with professors like Jeff Bishop, whose work, like that of Michael and Tracy Balboni, has deeply influenced my views in this book. The medical school at Loyola University-Chicago (also a Jesuit institution) also has a strong relationship with graduate programs in health-care ethics. One of the most exciting, a master's program in Health Care Mission Leadership, is run by a Catholic theologian, Therese Lysaught. Duke University offers formal theological formation for all students called to health care. It is offered to medical students from Duke or any other medical school between their third and fourth years. The Health, Spirituality, and Religion Program at the University of Michigan's medical school continues to grow in importance as a crossroads of medicine and theology. Kristin Collier, a professor of internal medicine and director of the program, notes that they have just begun collecting data through qualitative interviews, but the early responses from students are encouraging:

> "The Health, Spirituality and Religion Lecture Series has brought in captivating speakers who have contextualized how religion and spirituality are intertwined with the health of patients. Hearing about the personal experiences of these health-care providers has helped me develop a foundation as a medical student that motivates me to care for and honor the whole person during my clinical rotations."

"I have grown in my ability to care for the whole patient through participating in the Health, Spirituality and Religion Program."

"I have found incredibly valuable mentorship in the Health, Spirituality and Religion Program. Connecting with faculty members who are personally motivated by spirituality and religion in their practice of medicine has inspired me to reflect on how that holds true for myself and how I can best support patients and other health-care professionals who find that religion and spirituality are central to their wellbeing."

Michigan Medicine has also seen significant growth in its clinical pastoral education (CPE) program. It now has an accredited CPE residency with interns and residents who have expanded the chaplaincy footprint at the teaching hospital for a top-10 medical school and increased the opportunities for inter-professional care and attending to the spiritual needs of their patients.

Conclusion

So while there is a long way to go, these examples (and there are more I didn't have space to mention) can ground reasonable hope that much can be accomplished in this medium-term timeframe. After that, especially when the numbers of those with late-stage dementia begin to rise even more dramatically, different strategies may be necessary if sufficient change has not begun. But that difficult scenario raises an important question, especially for my fellow Christians in the United States and other Western countries: *How ready are we to cast out into the deep and engage in this essential dialogue?*

Can we stop being embarrassed about our religious beliefs in public contexts and respectfully but firmly request an equal seat at the table of dialogue? Can we look for overlapping consensus, but refuse to translate our views (using someone else's moral language) into a milquetoast version of what we actually believe in our hearts? Now is not the time to be arrogant and dismissive, but it also is not a time to be hesitant and timid. In the introduction we saw that even secular giants like Habermas accept that Christian theology lies at the root of fundamental human equality. And as David Bentley Hart points out, the concept of human dignity was quite a rare thing in the West before Christianity became culturally influential.[262] David Lantigua showed us that Christian notions of human equality led to the West's understanding of universal human rights. We should enter these dialogues with hope and confidence that on our own terms and without fear we have something essential to say to the culture in defense of fundamental human equality.

Conclusion

And What If We Fail?

What happens if, after about a decade or so, not much has changed? (Or, God forbid, things get even worse?) If cultural change isn't on the way, I propose that religious organizations and institutions mobilize for a massive, all-hands-on-deck response of our own. Speaking from my own perspective as a Catholic Christian, I can say that—while the task is daunting—not only does the Church have the international reach to mobilize for such a response, but this work would also be consistent with our history of responding to the signs of the times. Indeed, in some ways this is precisely the problem that a massive, transnational, multi-millennial religious institution is called to address.

Recall from chapter 1 some of what we learned about the historical relationship between the Church and health care. Some scholars even believe that the Church's response to health-care disasters helped it grow from a small and strange sect into a dominant cultural force. The first hospitals came from the Church and from the emphasis of certain religious orders on health care. The Benedictines insisted that care of the sick must be put before *everything* else. Sometimes whole new orders came into being specifically to deliver health care. The order of Knights Hospitaller was founded, at least at first, in association with an eleventh-century hospital in Jerusalem to provide health care for the sick, injured, and poor Christians on pilgrimage to the Holy Land. (Interestingly, this order evolved into the Order of Malta, which still continues its health-care work globally.[263]) Sometimes the Church mobilized to meet local outbreaks of disease. To deal with people who had leprosy, for instance, the Church created hospitals specifically for lepers (called leprosariums) and whole congregations emerged devoted to those suffering from the outbreak. The National Library of Medicine at the National Institutes of Health has exhibits dedicated to remembering "The Saints of the Plague" who served people during health-care emergencies.[264]

In the last three centuries, orders of women religious have taken the lead in setting up hospitals all over North America[265]—including, as we saw in chapter 1, during key moments of health-care crises. It began with an Augustinian nun named Marie Guenet de Saint-Ignace, who immigrated to Quebec in the mid-seventeenth century with the goal of establishing a Catholic hospital. She founded Quebec's Hôtel-Dieu, beginning the tradition of women's religious orders providing free no-strings-attached medical care in North America. The Sisters of Mercy and Daughters of Charity are among a dozen religious orders who served the United States during the Civil War, and in the process built the foundation for what would become the infrastructure of US health care.

Catholic orders of women religious mobilized around health-care education as well, founding approximately 220 nursing schools by 1915. In doing so these sisters "stamped their distinct understanding of nursing onto secular society."[266] And that imprint has endured: for instance, I recently gave a talk at Mercy College of Health Sciences in Des Moines, Iowa, which was founded as a nursing school by the Sisters of Mercy in 1899.[267]

In addition to administering hospitals and schools, contemporary women's religious orders are still doing direct work in health-care fields for the most vulnerable. A feature story in *The Atlantic*, "Nuns vs. the Coronavirus," detailed the selfless service many US religious women have given to the elderly and disabled in nursing homes during the 2020 pandemic.[268] Beyond the pandemic, there are many different religious orders geared toward the very issues I've raised in this book. An obvious example that comes to mind is the Little Sisters of the Poor, founded to serve the impoverished elderly who are thrown away at the end of their lives. Another important contemporary example is the Sisters of Life. Conceived by Cardinal John O'Connor of New York in the 1980s during a major health catastrophe, the order is called "to protect and enhance the sacredness of human life."[269] O'Connor had abortion primarily in mind, and the sisters have done and continue to do amazing work counseling and housing pregnant women in vulnerable and difficult situations.

But there is another health catastrophe related to the sacredness of human life on the horizon in the United States and around the world. Again, especially as human beings live longer, the number of people with late-stage dementia will continue to grow—in fact, the numbers will double about every twenty years if a cure is not found[270]—and there will be tremendous pressure within our consumerist throwaway culture to declare them human non-persons and make the problem go away. Assuming that efforts at dialogue over the next decade do not bear fruit, religious groups like the Catholic Church will have to mobilize to house, feed, and otherwise show hospitality to this extraordinarily vulnerable population.

Orders like the Sisters of Life and Little Sisters of the Poor no doubt will rise to meet the challenge in even greater numbers as the massive need becomes clear. But other religious orders will certainly need to retool their missions. We may need to resurrect orders from the Church's past that did similar work, like the Order of Widows.[271] Brand new orders will likely need to be created, as has happened throughout centuries past. And of course, we will need many more vocations to the religious life, including lay religious life, especially from larger religious families.[272]

Hundreds and hundreds of new hospitals and clinics, along with thousands of nursing homes, will need to be built and maintained. And if the surrounding culture is hostile to our understanding of fundamental human equality, we must be prepared—again, as we have been in the past—to build institutions that resist its practices. Here I have in mind what I hope does not turn out to be an eerie comparison to how a significant number of German Catholics resisted the Nazis' euthanasia program aimed at *Lebensunwertes Leben*, or "life unworthy of life." Recall from chapter 2 that it was this comparison which awoke Dr. Shewmon to the terrible reality of what was being done to human beings thought to be brain dead. Indeed, given what we have explored in this book, it is worth wondering why nearly 50 percent of physicians (a much higher proportion than any other profession) joined the Nazi party and why they were seven times more likely than other employed German males to join the SS.[273] Ashley K. Fernandes points these statistics out with a deep concern for our current moment in medicine—one in which he sees a new and ominous focus on "the state," "public health," and "quality of life" over the good and radical equality of all human beings. Nazi physicians, disturbingly, were eager to move from "doctor of the individual to doctor of the nation." Fernandes has reason to worry that we are moving in this direction again.

Like the German resistance of that day, our hospitals and other health-care institutions must be ready to resist. Perhaps we can look to the example of Cardinal Clemens August von Galen, who inspired such public backlash that the Nazis ended up abandoning their program of euthanasia for disabled adults. According to the historian Richard J. Evans, nurses and orderlies, especially in Catholic institutions for the sick and the disabled, were able "seriously to obstruct the process of registration."[274] Sister Anna Bertha Königsegg, a member of the Congregation of the Sisters of Mercy of St. Vincent de Paul, was one of the most important leaders of the resistance against the forced sterilizations and euthanasia of the disabled.[275] She was arrested by the Gestapo, and later the whole Congregation had their property confiscated throughout the Reich, but the general resistance they embodied was effective. Our own Christian health-care institutions must be prepared to resist in similar ways: nurses never registering the disabled for euthanasia, religious orders refusing to cooperate even if the government confiscates their property, and local bishops (along with other church leaders) inspiring the people to rise up in defense of fundamental human equality.

Our institutions must also pay the professional staff who care for this population (including home care staff) a living wage—a commitment that will require substantial outlays. Catholics and Protestants must, therefore, put aside differences and pool many different kinds of resources to meet the challenge. Such support must come not only from the hierarchical leadership, but also from the bottom up: with local parishes and churches setting up programs by which parishioners will go to work in local facilities and visit with residents, take them on walks, help at meals, and treat them with the fundamental human equality they deserve. We will also need to cooperate with our fellow people of the book, Muslims and Jews, and with all those committed to being a countercultural light in the darkness of a society that disregards or even undermines fundamental human equality.

If you're thinking that such a gargantuan undertaking might require a new religious revival, especially in the secularized consumerist West, I suspect you're right. And perhaps it sounds like wishful thinking, but I do wonder if our looming catastrophe might actually motivate such a revival. Great people in our Church's past, after all, began their lives caught in the trap of consumerism, but escaped to serve the most vulnerable during health-care emergencies. During the first stages of the COVID-19 pandemic, the president of Fordham University, Fr. Joseph McShane, S.J., sent our entire university community weekly pastoral messages. On Sunday, May 29, for instance, he sent us a note about how he had wept before a stained-glass window in the campus church depicting St. Aloysius Gonzaga receiving his First Communion from St. Charles Borromeo, the Archbishop of Milan. The story he related of "St. Al" is worth quoting at some length:

> Aloysius was the eldest son of the Marquis of Castiglione. Therefore, to say that he was a child of privilege would be an understatement. A vast understatement. A budding prince-ling, Aloysius spent his early life among the courtiers of the noble houses of Renaissance Italy (those hotbeds of ambition, corruption, intrigue and power), with a few side trips to the Hapsburg courts of Spain and Austria. Although he was destined to inherit his father's title and live a life of privilege, his head was not turned by what he saw in those settings. Far from it. In fact, he was deeply troubled by the venality and corruption he encountered in them and decided at an early age to enter the newly-founded Society of Jesus. His father was furious. Aloysius stood his ground. He renounced his titles and his inheritance and left behind him the life his father wanted for him. After he entered the Jesuits, he pursued his studies at the Roman College, where St. Robert Bellarmine was his spiritual director. When a plague broke out in Rome, like many of his young Jesuit confreres, he worked in the city's

hospitals, ministering to its victims. When his superiors (for fear of incurring his father's wrath) forbade him to continue his work, he pleaded with them to allow him to continue. They relented, but with a catch. They told him that he could only work in a hospital that did not serve contagious patients. He accepted the assignment on the spot. In the course of his service, however, he cared for a patient who had, in fact, been infected with the plague and was himself infected. He died shortly thereafter. His brethren recognized his holiness. They recognized his heroism. They recognized his goodness. They were also astounded by the magnitude of the sacrifices he had made: giving up the life of a courtier to live a life of simplicity, and giving up his life to serve the suffering. (His old spiritual director, Robert Bellarmine, a saint, a scholar, and a cardinal, was so impressed by Aloysius that he asked to be buried at his feet.) Throughout his life and in the manner of his death, then, Aloysius was a "sign of contradiction" (or a living oxymoron): he was a humble noble.

Millions and millions of people in the consumerist West are spiritually adrift, vocationally frustrated, addicted to empty practices of buying and selling, mortally lonely, and looking for meaning in their lives. Is it outrageous to think that dozens of millions of lukewarm or fallen-away Christians of various stripes will be deeply troubled by the "venality and corruption" of their daily lives and, amid a cultural emergency, come to grips with the importance of religious faith for the broader culture in which they live?[276] Wouldn't the millions of human beings with late-stage dementia, at risk of being discarded as mere things, also tug at the spiritual heartstrings of traditional believers who are not active in living out their faith?[277] And wouldn't the massive mobilization efforts themselves—perhaps like the efforts of the early Church described in chapter 1—be similarly attractive to new converts? Some, no doubt, would decide to enter newly founded religious orders. What energy, what hope, such a movement could bring! How much it could build! How many it could serve! It would truly be the light of Christ shining in a terrible darkness.[278]

But we haven't yet reached the final stage of the terrible darkness. Over the coming decade the medium-term goal of dialogue across differences on these issues can and should be pursued with high energy. If we can rekindle a broad cultural fire in defense of fundamental human equality, that would obviously be the better option. And don't forget the short-term goals, many of which we can work toward immediately as individuals and families.

And here, ending on a note of immediate action, I give Sacred Scripture the last word:

> My child, help your father in his old age,
> and do not grieve him as long as he lives;
> even if his mind fails, be patient with him;
> because you have all your faculties do not
> despise him.

For kindness to a father will not be forgotten,
and will be credited to you against your sins;
in the day of your distress it will be remem-
bered in your favor;
like frost in fair weather, your sins will melt
away.

(Sirach 3:12–15)

Endnotes

1. One might understandably question what I mean here by "secular" as a descriptor of philosophers. Aren't all philosophers secular? Well, no, there are plenty of Christian philosophers, for instance, whose focus is the philosophy of religion. This was my initial training as an undergraduate, with a senior thesis that used philosophy to think through what seems like the logical contradiction of the Trinity. Some philosophers bring specifically Christian ideas and traditions to bear in their work on other matters (including ethics and bioethics) while others do not or are even hostile to such ideas and traditions. It is true, however, that most philosophers—especially when debating each other—tend to appeal almost exclusively to "reason" (as opposed to revelation) and some would describe this perspective as secular. I will say more about how I'm using this term, and others related to it, in chapter 1.

2. While it is widely known that not all of the founders were Christians, they all believed that fundamental human equality came from being created that way by God. Thomas Jefferson, himself a deist, let this belief come through quite clearly in his drafting of the Declaration of Independence.

3. Indeed, some of the philosophers one might appeal to in favor of equality (say, Immanuel Kant and John Locke) argue not for human equality, but this kind of "trait X" notion of *personal* equality. Far from being supporters of fundamental human equality, they are two of the most important thinkers responsible for our cultural diversion into discussions of personal equality.

4. Admittedly, some make the distinction for other reasons as well—so that personhood and equality may be open to those beyond human beings. I'm one of them. See note 9 below for more.

5. David Lantigua, "On the Catholic Origins of Human Rights," May 23, 2016, https://churchlifejournal.nd.edu/articles/the-new-evangelization-in-the-americas-on-the-catholic-origins-of-human-rights/.

6. Jürgen Habermas, *Time of Transitions*, ed. and trans. C. Cronin and M. Pensky (Cambridge: Polity, 2006), 150–51.

7. Here are two more words I'm invoking beyond "secular": *secularized* and *irreligious*. Again, I will say more about them in chapter 1.

8. "Facts and Figures," Alzheimer's Association, https://www.alz.org/alzheimers-dementia/facts-figures#prevalence.

9. Those who are familiar with my previous work might find it strange that I focus on human equality here, especially given that I'm quite interested in rejecting theological speciesism. By focusing on *Homo sapiens* in this book, I'm not at all ruling out the possibility that other kinds of creatures are substances of a rational and relational nature. Angels, for instance, have this kind of nature. Perhaps some alien species with which we are unfamiliar also has one. Some non-human animals on earth (like whales, elephants, and gorillas) at the very least come close to sharing in this nature. But in this book I'm exclusively focused on the fact that all *Homo sapiens* share in this nature.

10. For example, see Kimbell Kornu, "Medical *Ersatz* Liturgies of Death: Anatomical Dissection and Organ Donation as Biopolitical Practice," in *Heythrop Journal - A BiMonthly Review of Philosophy and Theology*, doi:10.1111/heyj.13574.

11. Rodney Stark, *The Rise of Christianity: A Sociologist Reconsiders History* (Princeton, NJ: Princeton University Press, 1996).

12. J.J. Walsh, "Hospitals," *The Catholic Encyclopedia* (New York: Robert Appleton Company, 1910), retrieved from New Advent, http://www.newadvent.org/cathen/07480a.htm.

13. Roy Porter, *The Greatest Benefit to Mankind: A Medical History of Humanity from Antiquity to the Present* (New York; London: Harper Collins, 1997), 112.

14. Andrew T. Crislip, *From Monastery to Hospital: Christian Monasticism and the Transformation of Health Care in Late Antiquity* (Ann Arbor, MI: University of Michigan Press, 2005).

15. Walsh, "Hospitals."

16. "Our History," Filles du St. Esprit, 2017, https://www.fillesstesprit.org/site/english/716.html.

17. Tim McHugh, "Expanding Women's Rural Medical Work in Early Modern Brittany: The Daughters of the Holy Spirit," *Journal of the History of Medicine and Allied Sciences* 67, no. 3 (July 2012): 428–56.

18. Suzy Farren, "The Sister Nurses," *Health Progress* (March/April 2003), https://www.chausa.org/publications/health-progress/article/march-april-2003/the-sister-nurses.

19. "Our History," Daughters of the Holy Spirit, USA Province, 2018, https://daughtersoftheholyspirit.org/our-history/.

20. Kiley Bense. "We Should All Be More like the Nuns of 1918," *New York Times,* March 20, 2020, https://www.nytimes.com/2020/03/20/opinion/coronavirus-nuns.html.

21. Staff, "Catholic hospitals comprise one quarter of the world's healthcare, council reports," *Catholic News Agency,* February 10, 2010, https://www.catholicnewsagency.com/news/catholic_hospitals_represent_26_percent_of_worlds_health_facilities_reports_pontifical_council.

22. "Catholic Health Care in the United States," Catholic Health Association of the United States, https://www.chausa.org/about/about/facts-statistics.

23. Anna Maria Barry-Jester and Amelia Thomson-DeVeaux, "How Catholic Bishops Are Shaping Health Care in Rural America," *FiveThirtyEight (ABC News),* July 25, 2018, https://fivethirtyeight.com/features/how-catholic-bishops-are-shaping-health-care-in-rural-america/.

24. Charles Curran, "The Catholic Moral Tradition in Bioethics," in *The Story of Bioethics: From Seminal Works to Contemporary Explorations,* Jennifer K. Walter and Eran P. Klein, eds. (Washington, DC: Georgetown University Press, 2003), 113.

25. Daniel Callahan, *In Search of the Good: A Life in Bioethics* (Cambridge, MA: MIT Press, 2012), 67–69.

26. Such anger was more recently expressed by Ronald Green when he criticized the National Bioethics Advisory Commission (NBAC) for inviting religious panelists to comment on US policy concerning human embryonic stem cell research and cloning. See Ronald M. Green, *The Human Embryo Research Debates* (Oxford: Oxford University Press, 2001).

27. Tom L. Beauchamp and James F. Childress, *Principles of Biomedical Ethics,* 8th ed. (New York: Oxford University Press, 2019).

28. Joseph Tham, "The Secularization of Bioethics: A Critical Study," (PhD diss., Rome: Ateneo Pontificio Regina Apostolorum, 2007).

29. Albert Jonsen, "A History of Religion and Bioethics," *Handbook of Bioethics and Religion* (New York: Oxford University Press), 34.

30. It is true that ASBH accepts proposals from philosophers who write with some interest in religious ideas at a higher rate than what I suggest here. But here I'm primarily concerned with explicitly theological arguments. As I mention in a forthcoming article on the secularization of bioethics for

the *Journal of Medicine and Philosophy*, a colleague of mine in moral theology, new to bioethics, thought I must be wrong about this and decided to test it informally. He submitted one abstract in which he translated out the theological content and one with explicit theological content. ASBH accepted the first proposal and rejected the second. It was only the third time in his twenty-plus-year career that he had had a proposal rejected.

31. Timothy Murphy, "In Defense of Irreligious Bioethics," *American Journal of Bioethics* 12, (2012): 3-10.

32. In fact, though at the time this book goes to press it has not yet been published, the *Journal of Medicine and Philosophy* is poised to devote an entire issue to responding to Murphy's arguments.

33. Michael McCarthy, Mary Homan, and Michael Rozier (2020) "There's No Harm in Talking: Re-Establishing the Relationship Between Theological and Secular Bioethics," *The American Journal of Bioethics*, 20:12, 5–13, DOI: 10.1080/15265161.2020.1832611

34. R. Smith, R., and J. Blazeby, "Why Religious Belief Should Be Declared as a Competing Interest," *The BMJ* (Online) 361 (2020), doi:10.1136/bmj.k1456.

35. Kristen Collier, Twitter Post, August, 21, 2020, 9:22 AM, https://twitter.com/KristinCollie20/status/1289552042000650241.

36. Ruth Macklin, "Dignity is a Useless Concept," *The BMJ* 327, no. 7429 (December 20, 2003): 1419–1420.

37. Steven Pinker, "The Stupidity of Dignity," *The New Republic*, May 28, 2008, https://newrepublic.com/article/ 64674/the-stupidity-dignity.

38. Udo Schuklenk, "Professionalism Eliminates Religion as a Proper Tool for Doctors Rendering Advice to Patients," *Journal of Medical Ethics* 45, no. 11 (2019): 713.

39. Wesley J. Smith, "Bioethics Intends to Destroy Catholic Healthcare," *National Review*, September 16, 2019, https://www.nationalreview.com/corner/bioethics-intends-to-destroy-catholic-healthcare/.

40. Ronit Y. Stahl and Ezekiel J. Emanuel, "Physicians, Not Conscripts—Conscientious Objection in Health Care," *The New England Journal of Medicine,* April 6, 2017, https://www.nejm.org/doi/full/10.1056/NEJMsb1612472.

41. Rachel Browne, "Medical schools should deny applicants who object to provide abortion, assisted death: bioethicist," *Global News*, November 23,

2019, https://globalnews.ca/news/6183548/medical-school-applicants-abortion-assisted-death-conscientious-objectors/.

42. Wesley J. Smith, "Obliged to Kill," *The Washington Examiner*, March 2, 2018, https://www.washington examiner.com/weekly-standard/obliged-to-kill.

43. Caroline Kelly, "Medical center's federal funding threatened after nurse says she was forced to participate in an abortion," *CNN*, August 28, 2019, https://www.cnn.com/2019/08/28/politics/hhs-notice-of-violation-vermont-nurse-abortion/index.html.

44. Brigitte Amiri, "The Federal Government Must Stop Catholic Hospitals From Harming More Women," ACLU, last modified May 24, 2016, https://www.aclu.org/blog/reproductive-freedom/religion-and-reproductive-rights/federal-government-must-stop-catholic.

45. Ian D. Wolfe and Thaddeus M Pope, "Hospital Mergers and Conscience-Based Objections - Growing Threats to Access and Quality of Care," *The New England Journal of Medicine* 382 (15): 1388–89.

46. Callahan, 68.

47. Jonathan B. Imber, *Trusting Doctors: The Decline of Moral Authority in American Medicine* (Princeton, NJ: Princeton University Press, 2008).

48. Michael J. Balboni and Tracy A. Balboni, *Hostility to Hospitality: Spirituality and Professional Socialization within Medicine* (New York: Oxford University Press, 2019), 32.

49. It is worth noting that there has been an improvement in the relationship between medicine, ethics, and the humanities broadly speaking. Indeed, the most important annual bioethics conference is the meeting of the American Society of Bioethics *and Humanities*. But this has not made connections between bioethics and religion stronger. Indeed, the contemporary humanities may be even *more* secularized and irreligious than clinically-focused bioethics.

50. Balboni and Balboni, 100.

51. Jeffrey P. Bishop, *The Anticipatory Corpse: Medicine, Power, and the Care of the Dying* (Notre Dame, IN: University of Notre Dame Press, 2011).

52. Browne, "Medical schools should deny."

53. This becomes especially clear when one considers the nature of a clinical ethics consult. See Abram Brummett, "The Quasi-religious Nature of Clinical Ethics," *HEC Forum: HealthCare Ethics Committee Forum: An Interprofessional Journal on Healthcare Institutions' Ethical and Legal Issues* (2002): 1–11, doi: 10.1007/s10730-019-09393-5.

54. Sydney Lupkin, "Why Jahi McMath's Mom Is Sure Her Daughter Isn't Brain Dead," *ABC News*, December 16, 2014, https://abcnews.go.com/Health/jahi-mcmaths-mom-daughter-brain-dead/story?id=27570953.

55. Staff, "Portugal baby born to woman brain dead for three months," *BBC News*, March 29, 2019, https://www. bbc.com/news/world-europe-47741343. This is one example, but the sheer number of times this has happened is extraordinary. For a review of the cases before 2010 see Majid Esmaeilzadeh, Christine Dictus, Elham Kayvanpour, et al., "One life ends, another begins: Management of a brain-dead pregnant mother-A systematic review-" *BMC Medicine* 8, no. 74 (2010), https://doi.org/10.1186/1741-7015-8-74.

56. These details come from Rachel Aviv's 2018 *New Yorker* article on Jahi's story. Details from her story relayed below, until the discussion on racial justice, come from Aviv's skillful reporting as well, unless otherwise cited. Rachel Aviv, "What Does It Mean to Die?" *New Yorker*, January 29, 2018, https://www.newyorker.com/ magazine/2018/02/05/what-does-it-mean-to-die.

57. Paul Elias, "Judge opens door for lawsuit over girl declared brain dead," *Associated Press*, September 7, 2017, https://apnews.com/0721c8594d0143ecb731ba890b87077c/Judge-opens-door-for-lawsuit-over-girl-declared-brain-dead.

58. Yolonda Wilson, "Why the case of Jahi McMath is important for understanding the role of race for black patients," *The Conversation*, July 12, 2018, https://theconversation.com/why-the-case-of-jahi-mcmath-is-important-for-understanding-the-role-of-race-for-black-patients-99353. For a deeper dive into this shameful history, readers may want to consult Harriet A. Washington, *Medical Apartheid: The Dark History of Medical Experimentation on Black Americans from Colonial Times to the Present* (New York: Harlem Moon, 2001). Also Rebecca Skloot, *The Immortal Life of Henrietta Lacks* (New York: Broadway Books, 2011).

59. Todd L. Savitt, "The Use of Blacks for Medical Experimentation and Demonstration in the Old South," *The Journal of Southern History* 48, no. 3 (August 1982): 331–48.

60. Katrina Armstrong, Karima L. Ravenell, Suzanne McMurphy, and Mary Putt, "Racial/Ethnic Differences in Physician Distrust in the United States." *American Journal of Public Health* 97, no. 7 (July 2007): 1283–89.

61. Gilbert C. Gee and Chandra L. Ford, "Structural Racism and Health Inequalities: Old Issues, New Directions," *Du Bois Review: Social Science Research on Race* 8, no. 1 (April 2011): 115–32.

62. Staff, "Disparities in Healthcare Quality Among Racial and Ethnic Minority Groups: Selected Findings From the 2010 National Healthcare Quality and Disparities Reports," Agency for Healthcare Research and Quality, last updated October 2014, https://archive.ahrq.gov/research/findings/nhqrdr/nhqrdr10/minority.html.

63. Pew Research Center, "Views on End-of-Life Medical Treatments: Growing Minority of Americans Say Doctors Should Do Everything Possible to Keep Patients Alive," Pew Forum, last updated November 21, 2013, https://www.pewforum.org/2013/11/21/views-on-end-of-life-medical-treatments/.

64. Sarah Varney, "Toward Hospice Care," *New York Times*, August 21, 2015, https://www.nytimes.com/2015/08/ 25/health/a-racial-gap-in-attitudes-toward-hospice-care.html.

65. Patricia King, "Address Inequalities before Legalizing Suicide," *New York Times*, April 10, 2012, https://www.ny times.com/roomfordebate/2012/04/10/why-do-americans-balk-at-euthanasia-laws/address-inequalities-before-legalizing-assisted-suicide.

66. Ken Murray, "How Doctors Die: It's Not Like the Rest of Us, But It Should Be," *Zócalo: Public Square (an ASU Knowledge Enterprise)*, last updated November 20, 2011, https://www.zocalopublicsquare.org/2011/11/30/how-doctors-die/ideas/nexus/.

67. John Wyatt, "End-of-life Decisions, Quality of Life and The Newborn," *Acta Pædiatrica* 96, no. 6 (May 24, 2007): 790–91.

68. Carlo V. Bellieni and Giuseppe Buonocore, "Flaws in the Assessment of the Best Interests of the Newborn," *Acta Pædiatrica* 98, no. 4 (March 6, 2009): 613–17.

69. Stefan Timmermans, "Social Death as Self-Fulfilling Prophecy: David Sudnow's *Passing On* Revisited," *The Sociological Quarterly* 39, no. 3 (June 1998): 453–72.

70. Saroj Saigal, Barbara L. Stoskopf, David Feeny, et al., "Differences in Preferences for Neonatal Outcomes Among Health Care Professionals, Parents, and Adolescents," *JAMA* 281, no. 21: 1991–97.

71. Linda Thrasybule, "Heart patients prefer longevity over quality of life," *Reuters*, November 25, 2011, https:// www.reuters.com/article/us-heart-patients-longevity/heart-patients-prefer-longevity-over-quality-of-life-idUSTRE7AO1UR20111126.

72. "Oregon's Death with Dignity Act—2014," annual report, Oregon Public Health Division, released February 2015, https://www.oregon.gov/

oha/PH/PROVIDERPARTNERRESOURCES/EVALUATIONRE-
SEARCH/DEATHWITH DIGNIT ACT/Documents/year17.pdf.

73. Bishop, *The Anticipatory Corpse*, 216.

74. Lupkin, "Why Jahi McMath's Mom Is Sure".

75. It takes us into deep metaphysical waters very quickly, but it is worth noting that some thinkers, including some Catholic thinkers, do think that *properly diagnosed* whole brain death is nevertheless still the death of the human being. Perhaps Jahi was diagnosed incorrectly, and while that's a practical and moral concern for medicine, that's not an argument for abandoning the whole brain death criteria for death in principle. Perhaps one should make a distinction between a brain integrating the function of the whole organism and the spinal cord or other mechanisms coordinating various functions like, say, infection resistance. It goes beyond the scope of this chapter to dive deeply into these arguments, but my basic reaction to them is twofold. First, each of us was a functioning, living human being prenatally before we had a brain that was capable of integrating the function of the whole organism—which means that such integration is not a necessary condition for fundamental human equality at the end of life either. Second, given the historical temptation we have faced—and given into—to discard and even kill certain human beings as non-persons (especially when it puts strains on our resources to decide a certain way) we ought to proceed with epistemic humility and err on the side of caution when it comes to thinking about the moral and legal status of human beings with catastrophic brain injuries. For more from Catholic thinkers with a different view, however, see Patrick Lee and Germain Grisez, "Total Brain Death: A Reply to Alan Shewmon," *Bioethics*, vol. 26, no. 5: 275–84 and Jason T. Eberl, "A Thomistic Defense of Whole-Brain Death," *The Linacre Quarterly* 82 (3): 235–50.

76. Lizzie Johnson, "Jahi McMath's family wins backing for argument that she's alive," *San Francisco Chronicle*, July 24, 2017, https://www.sfchronicle.com/bayarea/article/Jahi-McMath-s-family-wins-backing-for-argument-11319544.php.

77. Aviv, "What Does It Mean to Die?"

78. Staff, "Report: Jahi McMath's Brain Showed Some Signs of Improvement After Brain Death, Doctors Say," *CBS Sacramento*, July 3, 2018, https://sacramento.cbslocal.com/2018/07/03/jahi-mcmath-brain-death-report/.

79. Natalie Morales, transcript to "'Dead' man recovering after ATV accident," *Dateline NBC*, last updated March 24, 2008, https://www.nbcnews.com/id/wbna23768436#.XjiOMyNOmUm.

80. A.E. Walker, E.L. Diamond, and J. Moseley, "The neuropathological findings in irreversible coma: a critique of the 'respirator brain,'" *Journal of Neuropathology & Experimental Neurology* 34, no. 4 (July 1975): 295–323. It is worth noting, however, that when more care is taken to apply the criteria correctly the numbers of mistakes go down. See D.M. Greer, H.H. Wang, J.D. Robinson, et al., "Variability of Brain Death Policies in the United States," *JAMA Neurology* 73, no. 2 (February 2016): 213–18.

81. D. Alan Shewmon, "Truly Reconciling the Case of Jahi McMath," *Neurocritical Care* 29, no. 2 (October 2018): 165–60.

82. Arthur L. Caplan, "Misusing the Nazi Analogy," *Science* 309 (5734), 535. https://science.sciencemag.org/content/sci/309/5734/535.full.pdf

83. Associated Press, "Brain-dead woman gives birth, then dies," *NBC News*, last updated June 12, 2006, https://www.nbcnews.com/id/wbna13274978.

84. Helen MacDonald, "Crossing the Rubicon: Death in 'The Year of the Transplant,'" *Medical History* 61, no. 1 (January 2017): 107–27.

85. Henry K. Beecher, "Ethical Problems Created by the Hopelessly Unconscious Patient," *New England Journal of Medicine*, 78 (1968): 1425–30.

86. Peter Singer, *Rethinking Life and Death: The Collapse of Our Traditional Ethics* (New York: St. Martin's Press, 1995). See also Charles Camosy, *Peter Singer and Christian Ethics: Beyond Polarization* (Cambridge, UK: Cambridge University Press, 2012).

87. Bishop, *The Anticipatory Corpse*.

88. However, there are still diverse views from state to state and even hospital to hospital. This has caused members of the neurology community to push for a common brain death standard. In part because of the moral reasoning over why certain things (like a supposedly-dead girl getting her period) should or should not matter, it looks like a common standard will be difficult to come by. See Gina Shaw, "Dead in California, Alive in New Jersey: Neurologists Seek Nationwide Consistency in Policies for Determining Brain Death," *Neurology Today*, January 9, 2020, https://journals.lww.com/neurotodayonline/Fulltext/2020/01090/Dead_in_California,_Alive_in_New_Jersey_.7.aspx.

89. For more on these arguments, see chapter 2 of Camosy, *Peter Singer and Christian Ethics*.

90. Again, it goes beyond the scope of this book to get into the arguments. But in principle I think double effect allows one to engage in activity not

aimed at one's death (either as a means or end), but which merely foresees that the act is likely to result in one's death. A dramatic example of this can be found in Nick Cassavetes's 2002 film *John Q* (USA: New Line Cinema). Denzel Washington plays a Catholic factory worker who resorts to hostage-taking in a hospital to ensure that his underinsured son receives a life-saving heart transplant, essentially giving up his own freedom for his son's future. As this book goes to press, I'm working on an academic article which uses the John Q case in support of my position here.

91. This information comes from a phone conversation with Bobby Schindler on December 31, 2019. It is used here with his permission.

92. Matt Lauer, transcript, "Michael Schiavo's side of the story," *Dateline NBC,* last updated March 27, 2006, http://www.nbcnews.com/id/12025860/ns/dateline_nbc/t/michael-schiavos-side-story/#.XjjaqS-NOmUI.

93. Joshua E. Perry, "Biblical Biopolitics: Judicial Process, Biblical Rhetoric, Terri Schiavo and Beyond," *Health Matrix: Journal of Law Medicine* 16, no. 2 (2006): 553–630.

94. Congregation for the Doctrine of the Faith, "Responses to Certain Questions of the United States Conference of Catholic Bishops Concerning Artificial Nutrition and Hydration" (August 1, 2007), Holy See: Vatican Archive, http://www.vatican.va/roman_curia/congregations/cfaith/documents/rc_con_cfaith_doc_20070801_risposte-usa_en.html.

95. M. Johnson, "Terri Schiavo: a disability rights case," *Death Studies* 30, no. 2 (March 2006): 163–76.

96. Josie Byzek, "Articulating our perspective to progressives," *Ragged Edge Online,* March 25, 2005, http://www.raggededgemagazine.com/focus/byzekprogressives.html.

97. "Terri Marie Schiavo," Find A Grave, https://www.findagrave.com/memorial/10708617/terri-marie-schiavo.

98. Amy Davidson Sorkin, "The Punisher: Jeb Bush and the Schiavos," *New Yorker,* February 18, 2015, https:// www.newyorker.com/news/amy-davidson/learning-jeb-bush-terri-schiavo/amp.

99. Gregory A Petsko, "A matter of life or death," *Genome Biology* 6, no. 5 (2005): 109.

100. Wesley J. Smith, "Human Non-Person," *National Review*, March 29, 2005, https://www.nationalreview.com/2005/03/human-non-person-wesley-j-smith/.

101. It is true that there are times where we must take into account cost in ways that might make very, very expensive treatment extraordinary; but it is never acceptable to do so based on a negative judgment related to a patient's disability. I wrote a book about this: *Too Expensive to Treat?: Finitude, Tragedy, and the Neo-Natal ICU* (Grand Rapids, MI: Eerdmans, 2010).

102. Newsroom, "The cost of extending our lives," *The Denver Post*, April 12, 2006, https://www.denverpost.com/ 2006/04/12/the-cost-of-extending-our-lives/.

103. Tyler Cowen, "The economics of Terry Schiavo," *Marginal Revolution*, last updated March 28, 2005, https:// marginalrevolution.com/marginal-revolution/2005/03/the_forthcoming.html.

104. I do think there are deeply complex, necessary questions to ask about just allocation of scarce resources. I wrote about them in *Too Expensive to Treat? Finitude, Tragedy, and the Neonatal ICU*. In that book I'm at pains to show, however, that answers to such questions should take every precaution to make sure that problems we face in allocating health care justly never tempt us to think of certain human beings as less than equal.

105. Philipp Kellmeyer, review of *Rights Come to Mind: Brain Injury, Ethics, and the Struggle for Consciousness*, by Joseph J. Fins, *Cambridge Quarterly of Healthcare Ethics* 52 (2016): 738–40.

106. Joseph J. Fins, "Disorders of Consciousness, Past, Present and Future," *Cambridge Quarterly of Healthcare Ethics* 28 (2019): 603–19.

107. Joseph J. Fins, *Rights Come to Mind: Brain Injury, Ethics, and the Struggle for Consciousness* (Cambridge, UK: Cambridge University Press, 2015).

108. Joseph J. Fins, "When No One Notices: Disorders of Consciousness and the Chronic Vegetative State," *Hastings Center Report* 49, no. 4 (2019); 14–17.

109. Fins, *Rights Come to Mind*.

110. Fins, "When No One Notices."

111. Kirk Payne et al., "Physicians' Attitudes about the Care of Patients in the Persistent Vegetative State: A National Survey," *Annals of Internal Medicine* 125, no. 2 (1996): 104–10.

112. R. Hoffenberg et al., "Should organs from patients in permanent vegetable state be used for transplantation?" *Lancet* 350, no. 9087 (November 1, 1997): 1320–1.

113. Stephen Drake, "Maryland: Using a 'PVS' Diagnosis to justify Organ Harvesting Without Consent," Not Dead Yet: The Resistance, February

21, 2012, http://notdeadyet.org/2012/02/maryland-using-pvs-diagnosis-to-justify.html.

114. Henry K. Beecher, "Ethical Problems Created by the Hopelessly Unconscious Patient," *New England Journal of Medicine* 278 (1968): 1425–30.

115. I do think there is a sense in which we can speak of people with something approaching a zero percent chance (given current technology) of regaining consciousness as still having "potential" for it based on the kind of creature a human being is. That is, based on our nature. It requires getting into the philosophical weeds, however, and if readers are interested they might consider reading the first two chapters of my *Peter Singer and Christian Ethics* (Cambridge University Press, 2012).

116. Fins interestingly shows that it is precisely this Aristotelian understanding of the soul that was behind the original naming of the state as "vegetative," but that doesn't avoid the critique made by pro-lifers. Indeed, in some ways it makes it more explicit because Aristotle's metaphysical view of the person (which was basically adopted by St. Thomas Aquinas) is very much at the heart of my central critique. More on this in footnote 258 below and in chapter 7, in which I use this fact as the basis for possible dialogue across different views on personhood and human life going forward.

117. Cell Press, "After 15 years in a vegetative state, nerve stimulation restores consciousness," *Science Daily*, last updated September 25, 2017, https://www.sciencedaily.com/releases/2017/09/170925132935.htm.

118. Centuries of attempts from the some of the finest philosophers and biological researchers have failed to locate consciousness in the human brain. The prospects of doing so are so poor, in fact, that some have even moved to reject the very notion of human consciousness as an illusion. Thomas Nagel and Alva Noë, for instance, have demonstrated that a fully functioning, healthy brain is an inadequate explanation for fundamental aspects of human existence and cognition, including self-awareness. See Thomas Nagel, *Mind & Cosmos: Why the Materialist Neo-Darwin Conception of Nature Is Most Certainly False* (Oxford; New York: Oxford University Press, 2012). Nagel concludes that the materialist account of consciousness fails, and Noë in turn claims that human consciousness must be understood as an "embodied" function of the entire human organism, holistically considered. For more on this see especially Noë's book *Out of Our Heads: Why You Aren't Your Brain and Other Lessons from the Biology of Consciousness* (New York: Hill and Wang, 2009).

119. Fins, *Rights Come to Mind*, 124–25.

120. Norma McCorvey and Andy Meisler, *I Am Roe* (New York: HarperCollins, 1994), 131.

121. Ruth Graham, "How the Anti-Abortion Movement is Responding to Jane Roe's 'Deathbed Confession,'" *Slate,* May 22, 2020, https://slate.com/human-interest/2020/05/jane-roe-norma-mccorvey-confession-anti-abortion.html.

122. Jason Keyser, "Ginsburg says Roe gave abortion opponents target," *USA Today,* May 11, 2013, https://www.usatoday.com/story/news/nation/2013/05/11/ginsburg-abortion-roe-wade/2153083/.

123. Linda Greenhouse, "Misconceptions About Roe v. Wade," *New York Times,* January 23, 2019, http:// opinionator. blogs.nytimes.com/2013/01/23/misconceptions/?_r=0.

124. Noah Feldman, "A reminder: Physicians were the key to Roe v. Wade," *Charlotte Observer,* May 24, 2016, https://www.charlotteobserver.com/opinion/op-ed/article79596967.html/.

125. Jeffrey Toobin, "The People's Choice," *New Yorker,* January 21, 2013, https://www.newyorker.com/magazine/2013/01/28/the-peoples-choice-2.

126. Linda Greenhouse, *Becoming Justice Blackmun: Harry Blackmun's Supreme Court Journey* (New York: Times Books, 2005), 18.

127. David L. Garrow. *Liberty and Sexuality: The Right to Privacy and the Making of Roe V. Wade* (New York: MacMillan, 1994).

128. Clarke D. Forsythe, *Abuse of Discretion: The Inside Story of Roe v. Wade* (New York: Encounter Books, 2013).

129. R. A. Barber, "Criminal liability of physicians: an encroachment on the abortion right?" *The American Criminal Law Review* 18, no. 4 (Spring 1981): 591–615.

130. Sheri Fink, *Five Days at Memorial: Life and Death in a Storm-Ravaged Hospital* (New York: Crown Publishers, 2013).

131. *Doe v. Bolton,* 410 U.S. 179 (1973).

132. Ken I. Kersch, review of *Becoming Justice Blackmun: Harry Blackmun's Supreme Court Journey,* by Linda Greenhouse, *Commentary* (July/August 2005), https://www.commentarymagazine.com/articles/becoming-justice-blackmun-by-linda-greenhouse/.

133. Linda Greenhouse and Reva B. Siegel, "The Unfinished Story of *Roe v. Wade.*" in *Reproductive Rights and Justice Stories,* Melissa Murray, Katherine Shaw, and Reva B. Siegel, eds. (New York: Foundation Press, 2019), 53–76.

134. Paul R. Ehrlich, *The Population Bomb* (New York: Ballantine Books, 1968).

135. Forsythe, *Abuse of Discretion*, 168.

136. Bernard N. Nathanson, *The Hand of God: A Journey from Death to Life by the Abortion Doctor Who Changed His Mind* (Washington, DC: Regnery Publishing, 1996).

137. "Planned Parenthood pamphlet from 1952 admits Abortion 'kills the life of a baby,'" *Live Action*, May 17, 2017. https://www.liveaction.org/news/planned-parenthood-in-1952-abortion-kills-the-life-of-a-baby/.

138. "Alan F. Guttmacher Planned Parenthood interview, 1968," https://www.youtube.com/watch?v=G1pwA6onfR0&feature=emb_logo.

139. "U.S. Doctor Says Cubans Seek Birth Control Pills," *The Tuscaloosa News*, March 10, 1966, https://news.google.com/newspapers?nid=1817&dat=19660310&id=VW8hAAAAIBAJ&sjid=R4oFAAAAIBAJ&pg=7293,1556940.

140. Charles C. Camosy, "Pope Francis said it: Climate change is not a population crisis," *Crux*, August 24, 2016, https://cruxnow.com/commentary/2016/08/pope-francis-said-climate-change-not-population-crisis/.

141. Aaron Blake, "The most surprising part about the GOP's failed 20-week abortion ban push: It was popular," *Washington Post*, January 22, 2015, https://www.washingtonpost.com/news/the-fix/wp/2015/01/22/the-most-surprising-part-about-the-gops-failed-20-week-abortion-ban-push-it-was-popular/.

142. R. M. Farrell, H. Mabel, M. V. Reider, M. Coleridge, M. Yoder Katsuki, "Implications of Ohio's 20-Week Abortion Ban on Prenatal Patients and the Assessment of Fetal Anomalies," *Obstetrics and Gynecology* 129, no. 5 (May 2017): 795–99.

143. Brian Skotko, Susan Levine, and Richard Goldstein, "Self-perceptions from people with Down syndrome," *American Journal of Medical Genetics*, 155, no. 10 (2011): 2360–69.

144. Aaron Blake, "On Bernie Sanders, abortion and 'population control,'" *Washington Post*, September 5, 2019, https://www.washingtonpost.com/politics/2019/09/05/bernie-sanders-abortion-population-control/.

145. Dana Kozlov, "Woman Says Abortion Doctor Who Stored Fetal Remains Left Her Scarred," *CBS Chicago*, last updated September 19, 2019, https://chicago.cbslocal.com/2019/09/19/woman-says-abortion-doctor-who-stored-fetal-remains-left-her-scarred/.

146. *Planned Parenthood of Southeastern Pa. v. Casey*, 505 U.S. 833 (1992).

147. I spent extended time arguing that potential does matter, morally speaking, in the first two chapters of my book *Peter Singer and Christian Ethics: Beyond Polarization*. It comes, however, from the potential inherent in a human being's nature or the kind of creature they are, rather than from an acceptably-high percentage chance of achieving trait X.

148. Kristen Day and Charles Camosy, op-ed, "How the Democratic platform betrays millions of the party faithful," *Los Angeles Times*, July 25, 2016, https://www.latimes.com/opinion/op-ed/la-oe-day-and-camosy-democratic-platform-abortion-20160725-snap-story.html.

149. And it may come sooner rather than later. As I was reviewing a first draft of this manuscript, I came across a news story that Colorado had defeated a bill which would give the same legal protections and health care to babies who had been accidentally born in a botched abortion that those of a similar gestational age born in a more typical situation receive. See Valerie Richardson, "Colorado Dems defeat 'Born Alive' act requiring care for infants born after botched abortions," *Washington Times*, February 12, 2020, https://www.washingtontimes.com/news/ 2020/feb/12/born-alive-child-physician-relationship-act-colora/. Soon after that, a similar bill—despite having bipartisan support—was filibustered and defeated in the United States Senate. See Alexandra DeSanctis, "Democrats Block Born-Alive Abortion Survivors Protection Act in the Senate," *National Review*, February 25, 2020, https://www.nationalreview.com/corner/born-alive-abortion-survivors-protection-act-fails-in-the-senate/.

150 Ellen Roets, Sigrid Dierickx, Luc Deliens, et al, "Healthcare Professionals' Attitudes towards Termination of Pregnancy at Viable Stage." *Acta Obstetricia et Gynecologica Scandinavica*, August 2, 2020.

151. Claire Cain Miller, "Republicans Now Support a Form of Paid Leave: So What's the Holdup?" *New York Times,* November 21, 2019, https://www.nytimes.com/2019/11/21/upshot/paid-leave-2020-debate.html. Also see this brief filed in *Peggy Young v. United Parcel Service, Inc.*: https://aul.org/wp-content/uploads/2018/11/Brief-for-23-Organizations-in-Young-v.-UPS.pdf.

152. Jen Fulwiler, Twitter Post, January 18, 2020, 1: 14 PM, https://twitter.com/jenfulwiler/status/1086326029638090755?lang=en.

153. Natalie Kitroeff and Jessica Silver-Greenberg, "Pregnancy Discrimination Is Rampant Inside America's Biggest Companies," *New York Times*, June 15, 2018, https://www.nytimes.com/interactive/2018/06/15/business/pregnancy-discrimination.html?smid=tw-share.

154. Ann Clare Levy, "March for Life Unveils its 2020 Theme – Life Empowers: Pro-Life is Pro-Woman," March for Life, last updated October 15, 2019, https://marchforlife.org/march-for-life-unveils-its-2020-theme-life-empowers-pro-life-is-pro-woman/.

155. Genevieve Shaw Brown, "Mom and Baby With Down Syndrome Mail Letter to Doctor Who Suggested Abortion," *ABC News*, June 7, 2016, https://abcnews.go.com/Lifestyle/mom-baby-syndrome-mail-letter-doctor-suggested-abortion/story?id=39666410.

156. See M. T. Valenzuela, P. P. San-Martin, G. Cavada, "Is Abortion a Serious Health Problem in Chile in the Field of Maternal-Perinatal Health?," *Revista medica de Chile* 145, no. 8 (August 2017): 1013–20. See also: Staff, "FactCheck: Who's right about Ireland's record on maternal deaths?" *Thejournal.ie*, August 15, 2016, https://www. thejournal.ie/maternal-deaths-mortality-rate-ireland-pro-life-campaign-statistics-2921139-Aug2016/.

157. "Charlie's Law," Charlie Gard Foundation, https://www.thecharliegard foundation.org/charlies-law/.

158. Staff, "Bambino Gesù reiterates offer to care for Alfie Evans," *Vatican News*, April 19, 2018, https://www.vaticannews.va/en/vatican-city/news/2018-04/pope-francis-alfie-evans-bambino-gesu-mariella-enoc.html.

159. Pope Francis, Twitter Post, April 4, 2018, 2:56 PM, https://twitter.com/Pontifex/status/981606519702786048.

160. Alder Hey Children's NHS Foundation Trust v. Mr. Thomas Evans, Ms. Kate James, and Alfie Evans (A Child by His Guardian CAFCASS Legal) [2018] EWHC 308 (Fam).

161. "In the matter of Alvie Evans," summary of Court Order regarding permission to appeal application, the Supreme Court of the United Kingdom, last updated April 20, 2018, https://www.supremecourt.uk/news/permission-to-appeal-application-in-the-matter-of-alfie-evans.html.

162. Alder Hey Children's NHS Foundation Trust v. Mr. Thomas Evans, Ms. Kate James, and Alfie Evans.

163. Sean Morrison, "Alfie Evans update: Parents 'give severely ill toddler mouth to-mouth resuscitation' to keep him alive," *Evening Standard*, April 25, 2018, https://www.standard.co.uk/news/uk/alfie-evans-latest-parents-giving-severely-ill-toddler-mouth-tomouth-resuscitation-to-keep-him-alive-a3822741.html.

164. Alessandra Scotto di Santolo, "Alfie Evans update: 'It's INHUMANE!' Italian healthcare chief SLAMS NHS decision," *Express*, April 25, 2018,

https://www.express.co.uk/news/uk/950646/Alfie-Evans-update-Italian-NHS-court-case-latest-news.

165. Madlen Davies, "Parent's joy as toddler born with just 2% healthy brain tissue makes miraculous recovery, with scans showing the organ is fully functioning," *Daily Mail*, July 13, 2015, https://www.dailymail.co.uk/health/article-3159168/Parent-s-joy-toddler-born-just-2-healthy-brain-tissue-expected-not-survive-makes-miraculous-recovery-scans-showing-organ-fully-functioning.html.

166. Ferris Jabr, "Self-Awareness with a Simple Brain," *Scientific American*, November 1, 2012, https://www. scientificamerican.com/article/self-awareness-with-a-simple-brain/.

167. Michael A. Mancano, "Vigabatrin-Induced Encephalopathy; Fidaxomicin Hypersensitivity Reactions; Vemurafenib-Induced DRESS; Severe Alkalosis and Hypokalemia with Stanozolol Misuse; Isotretinoin-Associated Lip Abscess; Eltrombopag-Associated Hyperpigmentation," *Hospital Pharmacy* 49, no. 5 (May 2014): 420–24.

168. Alder Hey Children's NHS Foundation Trust v. Mr. Thomas Evans, Ms. Kate James, and Alfie Evans.

169. Matthew Shadle, "The Fatal Flaw in the Alfie Evans Decision," *Catholic Moral Theology* (blog), ed. David Cloutier and Jana Bennett, April 27, 2018, https://catholicmoraltheology.com/the-fatal-flaw-in-the-alfie-evans-decision/.

170. Christian Legal Centre, press release "Alfie Evans—emergency hearing today," *Christian Concern*, last updated April 24, 2018, https://christianconcern.com/ccpressreleases/alfie-evans-emergency-hearing-today/.

171. Samuel Osborne, "Alfie Evans 'still breathing' hours after life support was withdrawn, father says," *Independent*, April 24, 2018, https://www.independent.co.uk/news/uk/home-news/alfie-evans-life-support-latest-upodates-toddler-high-court-tom-evans-a8319401.html.

172. Charles C. Camosy, "Alfie Evans and Our Moral Crossroads," *First Things*, April 25, 2018, https:// www.firstthings.com/web-exclusives/2018/04/alfie-evans-and-our-moral-crossroads.

173. Charles C. Camosy, "Alfie Evans, Irreligion, and the Future of Bioethics," *Journal of Medicine & Philosophy* (forthcoming).

174. Josh Halliday, Twitter Post, April 24, 2018, 10:53 AM, https://twitter.com/joshhalliday/status/988808137594589184?lang=en.

175. Josh Halliday, "'Call from God': American pro-lifer's role in Alfie Evans battle," *The Guardian*, April 28, 2018, https://www.theguardian.com/uk-news/2018/apr/28/call-from-god-american-pro-lifers-role-in-alfie-evans-battle.

176. Janet Street-Porter, "What poor Alfie Evans needs now is peace and love, instead he has become a tragic pawn in a religious war," *Daily Mail*, April 25, 2018, http://www.dailymail.co.uk/news/article-5657149/JANET-STREET-PORTER-poor-Alfie-Evans-needs-peace-love.html.

177. Fleet Street Fox (Susie Boniface), "The so-called Christians hijacking Alfie Evans' last days are evil incarnate," *Daily Mirror*, April 25, 2018, https://www.mirror.co.uk/news/uk-news/called-christians-hijacking-alfie-evans-12424691.

178. Gaby Hinsliff, "Alfie Evans' parents needed help. The vultures came instead," *The Guardian*, April 26, 2018, https://www.theguardian.com/commentisfree/2018/apr/26/alfie-evans-parents-activists.

179. Nicholas Frankovich, "Alfie Evans, Post Mortem," *National Review*, April 28, 2018, https://www.national review.com/corner/alfie-evans-post-mortem/.

180. "NICE technology appraisal guidance," National Institute for Health and Care Excellence, https://www.nice.org.uk/about/what-we-do/our-programmes/nice-guidance/nice-technology-appraisal-guidance.

181. "Quality-adjusted life year," *Glossary*, National Institute for Heath and Care Excellence, https://www.nice.org.uk/Glossary?letter=Q#Quality-adjusted%20life%20year.

182. "Assessing cost effectiveness," from *Process and methods* [PMG6], in *The guidelines manual*, National Institute for Health and Care Excellence, last updated November 2012, https://www.nice.org.uk/process/pmg6/chapter/assessing-cost-effectiveness.

183. Stephen Barrie, "QALYs, euthanasia and the puzzle of death," *Journal of Medical Ethics* 41 (2015): 635–38.

184. NICE has numerous studies in its "economic evaluation database" which explicitly use QALYs when considering whether and how long to pay for ventilation for a patient.

185. Diane Coleman, "NCIL membership adopts resolution opposing Health Insurers' Use of QALYS," Not Dead Yet, http://notdeadyet.org/2020/08/ncil-membership-adopts-resolution-opposing-health-insurers-use-of-qalys.html.

186. Application for appeal before Lady Justice King, Lord Justice McFarlane, and Lord Justice McCombe, between E (A Child) [2018] EWCA Civ 550, pertaining to decision by Mr. Justice Hayden in Alder Hey Children's NHS Foundation Trust v. Mr. Thomas Evans, Ms. Kate James, and Alfie Evans (A Child by his Guardian CAFCASS Legal) [2018] EWHC 308 (Fam).

187. Thrasybule, "Heart patients prefer longevity."

188. John D. Lantos and William L. Meadow, "Should the 'Slow Code' Be Resuscitated?" *The American Journal of Bioethics* 11, no. 11 (2011): 8–12.

189. Natasha Hammond-Browning, "When Doctors and Parents Don't Agree: The story of Charlie Gard," *Journal of Bioethical Inquiry* 14. no. 4 (2017): 461–68.

190. "Tafida's triumph, and why it is not enough," *Christian Concern*, last updated October 25, 2019, https://christianconcern.com/comment/tafidas-triumph-and-why-it-is-not-enough/.

191. Sohrab Ahmari, "Pray that Charlie's Law is passed," *Catholic Herald*, June 20, 2019, https://catholicherald.co. uk/magazine/pray-that-charlies-law-is-passed/.

192. Haroon Siddique, "Legal attempt to keep girl alive not in her best interests, court told," *The Guardian*, September 10, 2019, https://www.theguardian.com/society/2019/sep/10/legal-bid-keep-girl-5-tafida-raqeeb-alive-against-best-interests-court-told.

193. Haroon Siddique, "Seriously ill girl can be taken to Italy for treatment, high court rules," *The Guardian*, October 3, 2019, https://www.theguardian.com/law/2019/oct/03/seriously-ill-girl-tafida-raqeeb-italy-treatment-high-court-rules.

194. Tafida Raqeeb (by her Litigation Friend XX) v. Barts NHS Foundation Trust, [2019] EWHC 2531 (Admin) and [2019] EWHC 2530 (Fam).

195. Rahila Gupta, op-ed "Does religion have a privileged status in the UK?" *CNN*, November 20, 2019, https://www. cnn.com/2019/11/20/opinions/rahila-gupta-religion-privileged-status-uk/index.html.

196. Hannah Brockhaus, "Tafida Raqeeb moved from intensive care unit in Italian hospital," *Catholic Herald*, January 9, 2002, https://catholicherald.co.uk/tafida-raqeeb-moved-from-intensive-care-unit-in-italian-hospital/.

197. Singer is a particular influence on me when it comes to my views on the moral status and treatment of non-human animals. That influence has led to these topics coming up in my work regularly—including in a book

titled *For Love of Animals: Christian Ethics, Consistent Action* (Cincinnati: Franciscan Media, 2013).

198. Michael Specter, "The Dangerous Philosopher," *New Yorker*, September 6, 1999, https://www.michaelspecter.com/1999/09/the-dangerous-philosopher/.

199. "The Challenge of Neurodegenerative Diseases," Harvard NeuroDiscovery Center, https://neurodiscovery.harvard.edu/challenge.

200. Alzheimer's Disease International, Summary sheet of *World Alzheimer Report 2015: The Global Impact of Dementia*, August 2015, https://www.alz.co.uk/research/WorldAlzheimerReport2015-sheet.pdf.

201. "African Americans and Alzheimer's Disease: The Silent Epidemic," Alzheimer's Association, https://www.alz.org/media/Documents/african-americans-silent-epidemic-r.pdf.

202. Press release, "Neurodegenerative Disease Market Research Report 2019: Global Industry Analysis, Business Development, Size, Share, Trends, Future Growth, Forecast to 2024," *MarketWatch*, last updated June 11, 2019, https://www.marketwatch.com/press-release/neurodegenerative-disease-market-research-report-2019-global-industry-analysis-business-development-size-share-trends-future-growth-forecast-to-2024-2019-06-11.

203. Fortune Business Insights, press release, "Neurodegenerative Diseases Drugs Market to Worth USD 62.7 Billion by 2026 | Global Industry Share and Growth Analysis by Top 10 Players," *Medgadget*, last updated September 17, 2019, https://www.medgadget.com/2019/09/neurodegenerative-diseases-drugs-market-to-worth-usd-62-7-billion

204. Sam Baker, "The outlook for Alzheimer's research keeps getting bleaker," *Axios*, March 25, 2019, https://www.axios.com/alzheimers-research-failure-start-over-biogen-9a379ee7-c163-413d-9853-9b66d7c1cb3e.html.

205. Alissa Sauer, "How Robots Could Help People With Dementia," *Alzheimers.net,* September 26, 2018, https://www.alzheimers.net/robots-could-help-people-with-dementia/.

206. Dennis Thompson, "Robots May Soon Become Alzheimer's Caregivers," *WebMD*, June 28, 2018, https://www. webmd.com/alzheimers/news/20180628/robots-may-soon-become-alzheimers-caregivers#1.

207. Sy Mukherjee, "This Adorable Robot Seal Helps Comfort Elderly Dementia Patients; Its Creator Just Won a $250,000 Prize," *Fortune*, October 12, 2018, https://fortune.com/2018/10/12/ryman-prize-paro-dementia-robot/.

208. Gregg A. Warshaw and Elizabeth J. Bragg, "Preparing the Health Care Workforce to Care for Adults with Alzheimer's Disease and Related Dementias," *Health Affairs* 33, no. 4 (April 2014), free access online, https://www.healthaffairs.org/doi/10.1377/hlthaff.2013.1232.

209. Robert Booth, "Robots to be used in UK care homes to help reduce loneliness," *The Guardian*, September 7, 2020, https://www.theguardian.com/society/2020/sep/07/robots-used-uk-care-homes-help-reduce-loneliness.

210 IOS Press, "Analysis reveals economic cost of Alzheimer's disease and dementia are 'tip of the iceberg,'" *ScienceDaily*, July 30, 2019, https://www.sciencedaily.com/releases/2019/07/190730092616.htm.

211. *2019 C.A.R.E. Study*, Northwestern Mutual, https://news.northwesternmutual.com/2019-care-study.

212. Baker, "The outlook for Alzheimer's research."

213. Though it is not specifically focused on dementia care, readers may benefit from consulting Harold Braswell's recent book, which addresses the burden on familial caregivers of patients approaching the end of life. See Harold Braswell, *The Crisis of US Hospice Care* (Baltimore, MD: Johns Hopkins University Press, 2019).

214. "Dementia—the true cost: Fixing the care crisis," Alzheimer's Society, https:/ www.alzheimers.org.uk/about-us/policy-and-influencing/dementia-true-cost-fixing-care-crisis.

215. National Council on Disability, "Quality-Adjusted Life Years and the Devaluation of Life with Disability," https://ncd.gov/sites/default/files/NCD_Quality_Adjusted_Life_Report_508.pdf, 50–51.

216. "Financial and Legal Planning for Caregivers: Medicare," Alzheimer's Association, https://www.alz.org/help-support/caregiving/financial-legal-planning/medicare.

217. "Policy Basics: Where Do Our Federal Tax Dollars Go?," Center on Budget and Policy Priorities, last updated January 29, 2019, https://www.cbpp.org/research/federal-budget/policy-basics-where-do-our-federal-tax-dollars-go.

218. Jeff Stein, "U.S. Government Debt Will Equal the Size of the Entire Economy for the First Time Since World War II," *Washington Post*, September 2, 2020, https://www.washingtonpost.com/us-policy/2020/09/02/government-debt-economy-coronavirus/.

219. Alan Rappeport, "Social Security and Medicare Funds Face Insolvency, Report Finds," *New York Times*, April 22, 2019, https://www.nytimes.

com/2019/04/22/us/politics/social-security-medicare-insolvency.html.

220. "Raise the Age of Eligibility for Medicare to 67," from *Options for Reducing the Deficit: 2019 to 2028*, Congressional Budget Office, last updated December 13, 2018, https://www.cbo.gov/budget-options/2018/54733.

221. Alzheimer's Disease International, Summary sheet of *World Alzheimer Report 2019: Attitudes to dementia*, September 2019, https://www.alz.co.uk/research/WorldAlzheimerReport2019-Summary.pdf.

222. "How at Risk for Abuse Are People with Dementia?" fact sheet, Center of Excellence on Elder Abuse and Neglect, Program in Geriatrics, University of California, Irvine, http://www.centeronelderabuse.org/docs/pwdementia_factsheet.pdf.

223. "Some Nursing Homes are Taking Resident's Stimulus Checks, FTC Warns," *CNN*, March 19, 2020. https://www.cnn.com/2020/05/19/us/stimulus-checks-nursing-home-theft-trnd/index.html

224. Dan W. Brock, "Justice and the Severely Demented Elderly," *The Journal of Medicine & Philosophy* 13, no. 1 (February 1988): 73–99.

225. Julian C. Hughes, *Thinking Through Dementia* (Oxford, UK; New York: Oxford University Press, 2011).

226. For more on this debate see Julian C. Hughes, Stephen J. Louw, and Steven R. Sabat, eds., *Dementia: Mind, Meaning, and the Person* (Oxford, UK; New York: Oxford University Press, 2006). See also Julian C. Hughes and Toby Williamson, *The Dementia Manifesto* (Cambridge, UK: Cambridge University Press, 2019) and Tom Kitwood, *Dementia Reconsidered, Revisited: The Person Still Comes First*, Dawn Brooker, ed. (London; New York: Open University Press 2019).

227. "Doctor Cleared of Murder in Euthanasia Case Says She Would Do It Again," *Dutch News*. June 15, 2020, https://www.dutchnews.nl/news/2020/06/doctor-cleared-of-murder-in-euthanasia-case-says-she-would-do-it-again/.

228. Daniel Boffey, "Dutch Euthanasia Rules Changed After Acquittal in Sedative Case," *The Guardian,* November 20, 2020, https://www.theguardian.com/world/2020/nov/20/dutch-euthanasia-rules-changed-after-acquittal-in-sedative-case.

229. Nicholas Goldberg, "Column: California's Aid-in-Dying Law is Working. Let's Expand it to Alzheimer's Patients," *Los Angeles Times*, July 15, 2020.

230 Human Rights Watch, "Using medicine in a wrong way for people with dementia in the United States," February 5, 2018, https://www.hrw.org/sites/default/files/accessible_document/they_want_docile_etr.pdf.

231. Jessica Silver-Greenberg and Amy Julia Harris, "'They Just Dumped Him Like Trash': Nursing Homes Evict Vulnerable Resident," *New York Times*, June, 21, 2020, https://www.nytimes.com/2020/06/21/business/nursing-homes-evictions-discharges-coronavirus.html.

232. University of Exeter, "Dementia gene raises risk of severe COVID-19," *ScienceDaily*, May 26, 2020, www.sciencedaily.com/releases/2020/05/200526091412.htm

233. CDC, "People with Certain Medical Conditions," https://www.cdc.gov/coronavirus/2019-ncov/need-extra-precautions/people-with-medical-conditions.html#neurologic-conditions.

234. Matt Sedensky and Bernard Condon, "Not just COVID: Nursing home neglect deaths surge in shadows," *Associated Press*, November 19, 2020, https://apnews.com/article/nursing-homes-neglect-death-surge-3b74a-2202140c5a6b5cf05cdf0ea4f32.

235. Tucker Doherty, "Summer Wave of Dementia Deaths Adds Thousands to Pandemic Deadly Toll," *Politico*, September 16, 2020, https://www.politico.com/news/2020/09/16/dementia-deaths-coronavirus-nursing-homes-416530.

236 Johnny Diaz, "Two Charged in Coronavirus Outbreak at Veterans' Home That Left 76 Dead," *New York Times*, September 25, 2020, https://www.nytimes.com/2020/09/25/us/veterans-home-holyoke-covid.html.

237 Taryn Luna, "Criticism Grows Over Gov. Gavin Newsom's Management of the Coronavirus Crisis," *Los Angeles Times*, April 29, 2020, https://www.latimes.com/california/story/2020-04-29/gavin-newsom-coronavirus-response-criticism-nonprofits-legislators.

238. Amy Silverman, "People with Intellectual Disabilities May Be Denied Lifesaving Care Under These Plans As Coronavirus Spreads," *ProPublica*, March 27, 2020, https://www.propublica.org/article/people-with-intellectual-disabilities-may-be-denied-lifesaving-care-under-these-plans-as-coronavirus-spreads.

239. U.S. Department of Health and Human Services, "OCR Reaches Early Case Resolution With Alabama After It Removes Discriminatory Ventilator Triaging Guidelines," April 8, 2020, https://www.hhs.gov/about/news/2020/04/08/ocr-reaches-early-case-resolution-alabama-after-it-

removes-discriminatory-ventilator-triaging.html.

240. Kim Painter, "Disabled N.J. girl thrives, inspires after transplant," *USA Today*, October 5, 2013, https://www. usatoday.com/story/news/nation/2013/10/05/disabled-transplant-amelia-rivera/2917989/.

241. John van Borsel, Sigrid de Grande, Griet van Buggenhout, Jean-Pierre Fryns, "Speech and language in Wolf-Hirschhorn syndrome: A case-study," *Journal of Communication Disorders* 37, no. 1 (February 2004): 21–33.

242. Charles C. Camosy, "COVID-19 Patient was Black and Paralyzed, So Doctors Decided His Life Wasn't Worth Saving," *New York Post*, July 10, 2020.

243. Joseph Shapiro, "As Hospitals Fear Being Overwhelmed by COVID-19, Do The Disabled Get The Same Access?," December 14, 2020, https://www.npr.org/2020/12/14/945056176/as-hospitals-fear-being-overwhelmed-by-covid-19-do-the-disabled-get-the-same-acc.

244. Joseph Shapiro, "Oregon Hospitals Didn't Have Shortages, So Why Were Disabled People Denied Care?," December 21, 2020, https://www.npr.org/2020/12/21/946292119/oregon-hospitals-didnt-have-shortages-so-why-were-disabled-people-denied-care.

245. Henry K. Beecher, "Ethical Problems Created by the Hopelessly Unconscious Patient," *New England Journal of Medicine* 278, no. 26 (June1968): 1425–30.

246. Corina Knoll, "Sweethearts Forever: Then Came Alzheimer's, Murder and Suicide," *New York Times,* December 29, 2019, https://www.nytimes.com/2019/12/29/nyregion/alzheimers-murder-suicide.html.

247. Charles C. Camosy, "Honoring the Elderly," *First Things*, July 26, 2020, https://www.firstthings.com/web-exclusives/2020/07/honoring-the-elderly.

248. Camosy, "Honoring the Elderly."

249. Jeffrey Bishop, *The Anticipatory Corpse.*

250. Brian Volck, "Bodies Without Ends," review of *The Anticipatory Corpse*, by Jeffrey Bishop, Syndicate, last updated October 27, 2014, https://syndicate.network/symposia/theology/the-anticipatory-corpse/.

251. Elaine Stratton Hild, "Medieval Rites and Contemporary Dying," *Church Life Journal*, April 27, 2018, https://churchlifejournal.nd.edu/articles/medieval-rites-and-contemporary-dying/.

252. Nicolas Diat, *A Time to Die: Monks on the Threshold of Eternal Life*, trans. Mary Dudro (San Francisco: Ignatius Press, 2019).

253. *Serving Life*, directed by Lisa Cohen, narrated by Forest Whitaker (Oprah Winfrey Network Documentary Club, 2011), film.

254. A.M., "The Burden Lifts: Caring for a Spouse Who Has Alzheimer's," *Living City* (February 2020), 12.

255. Stephanie Nolasco, "Sex Pistol Johnny Rotten on being a caretaker for his wife with dementia: 'The real person is still there,'" *Fox News*, June 8, 2020, https://www.foxnews.com/entertainment/sex-pistol-johnny-rotten-caretaker-nora-dementia.

256. Joseph Goldstein and Kevin Armstrong, "Could This City Hold the Key to the Future of Policing in America?," July 12, 2020, https://www.nytimes.com/2020/07/12/nyregion/camden-police.html.

257. Jonah McKeown, "George Floyd's Death Shows Need For 'Sanctity of Life' Police Training, Researcher Says," *Catholic News Agency*, June 7, 2020, https://www.catholicnewsagency.com/news/george-floyds-death-shows-need-for-sanctity-of-life-police-training-researcher-says-37676.

258. On this topic I've been influenced by two philosophers, Joe Vukov of Loyola University-Chicago and Charlie Lassiter of Gonzaga, who lay out this view in an article that, as this book goes to press, is currently under review. It argues that an Aristotelian view of powers entails (or at least fits incredibly well with) a 4E theory of cognition. The basic idea is that if you are an Aristotelian or Thomist in your metaphysics, then you probably shouldn't be reducing consciousness to brain activity. It is worth noting here that there are a number of other thinkers who have approached disability from an Aristotelian-Thomistic perspective, such as Miguel Romero, John Berkman, Richard Cross, Bryan Cross, and Kevin Timpe.

259. Given what I laid out in the first chapter of this book, one could understandably be puzzled as to why I think the discipline of bioethics may be open to this kind of dialogue. Significantly, just before this book went to press, the *American Journal of Bioethics* published a new issue with a target article titled "There's No Harm in Talking: Re-Establishing the Relationship Between Theological and Secular Bioethics" by Michael McCarthy, a theological bioethicist. See https://www.tandfonline.com/toc/uajb20/current. On the one hand, this issue of AJOB delivers bad news, for its operating assumption is that the relationship between theological and secular bioethics has been severed and several of the

responses to the target article argue that the relationship cannot and/or should not be reestablished. But on the other hand, there is good news to report as well. The fact that AJOB published the target article at all is a hopeful sign in itself. Also, the issue's editorial, from John Evans, gives a helpful set of thoughts on what a new dialogue might look like. He rightly points out that so much of bioethics is concerned with coming up with generalizable and calculable "rules" which could be readily adopted/enforced by bureaucratic committees as well as public/private managerial institutions. Evans bemoans the reduction of ethics to abstract principles (such as "autonomy") applied in service to research, health-care, or public institutions; he argues that a collaborative intervention on the part of theological bioethics within cultural bioethics—a subdiscipline not beholden to bureaucratic managers—can help to reintegrate these principles within a new bioethical conversation that takes theology seriously as a co-equal conversation partner. For more on Evans's broad vision, consider engaging his *Playing God? Human Genetic Engineering and the Rationalization of Public Bioethical Debate* (Chicago: University of Chicago Press, 2002).

260. Jeffrey P. Bishop, "Biopolitics, Terri Schiavo, and the Sovereign Subject of Death," *Journal of Medicine and Philosophy* 33 (2009): 538–57.

261. Balboni and Balboni, *Hostility to Hospitality*, 287.

262. David Bentley Hart, "Human Dignity Was a Rarity Before Christianity," *Church Life Journal*, October 26, 2017, https://churchlifejournal.nd.edu/articles/human-dignity-was-a-rarity-before-christianity/.

263. Sovereign Order of Malta, "Healthcare as a Fundamental Right," https://www.orderofmalta.int/humanitarian-medical-works/medical-facilities/.

264 Laura Hartman, "Remembering the Saints of the Plague," *U.S. National Library of Medicine*, November 1, 2020, https://circulatingnow.nlm.nih.gov/2019/11/01/remembering-the-saints-of-the-plague/.

265. Alicia Ambrosio, "Religious orders and health care a match made in heaven," Aleteia, August 26, 2017, https:// aleteia.org/2017/08/26/religious-orders-and-health-care-a-match-made-in-heaven/.

266. B. M. Wall, "Definite Lines of Influence: Catholic Sisters and Nurse Training Schools, 1890-1920." *Nursing Research* 50, no. 5 (September/October 2001): 314-21, https://pubmed.ncbi.nlm.nih.gov/11570717/.

267. I am deeply indebted to conversations I had there, especially with Bo Bonner, for windows into the Sisters of Mercy and the influence of women religious orders on health care more generally.

268. Emma Green, "Nuns vs. The Coronavirus," *The Atlantic,* May 3, 2020, https://www.theatlantic.com/politics/archive/2020/05/coronavirus-nursing-home-deaths/611053/.

269. "Who We Are: Made in His Image," Sisters of Life, https://sistersoflife.org/ who-we-are/who-we-are/.

270. And things do not look good on this front. The next new drug to treat Alzheimer's disease looks like it will be rejected by the Food and Drug Administration. See Laurie McGinley, "FDA advisers give thumbs-down to Alzheimer's drug, saying it lacks efficacy data," https://www.washingtonpost.com/health/2020/11/06/alzheimers-drug-fda-review/, November 6, 2020

271. M Therese Lysaught, "Practicing the Order of Widows: A New Call for an Old Vocation," *Christian Bioethics* 11, no. 1 (April 2005): 51–68.

272. As they stand right now, most religious orders are aging dramatically and quickly. While this is a weakness in terms of mobilizing for this kind of looming disaster, because religious orders themselves have been dealing with a crisis of aging, they will certainly have much to teach us in organizing our responses.

273. Ashley K. Fernandes, "Why Did So Many Doctors Become Nazis?," *Tablet,* December 9, 2020, https://www.tabletmag.com/sections/history/articles/ fernandes-doctors-who-became-nazis.

274. Richard J Evans, *The Third Reich At War* (New York: Penguin Press, 2009), 100.

275. Wolfgang Neugebauer, "The Nazi mass murder of the intellectually and physically disabled and the resistance of Sister Anna Bertha Königsegg," Lecture, Documentation Archive of the Austrian Resistance, Goldegg Castle, November 12, 1998, https://www.doew.at/cms/download/d7kv5/ wn_koenigsegg.pdf?fbclid=IwAR3-S8LENudyrMv7QvrIrhDKZZeM-pyLyoxwXkSw_MrdoL_ub-XXpE5WcaYA.

276. Indeed, we have some examples of this happening already. Consider the "Nuns and Nones" movement, an "alliance of Catholic sisters, spiritually diverse seekers, and other religious elders whose mission is to create communities of care and contemplation that incite courageous action." See "Our Story," Nuns & Nones, https://www.nunsandnones.org/about.

277. We saw hints of this, at least from my perspective, when it became clear that traditionally religious folks sustained our cultural alarm during the pandemic about what we were doing to our elders in nursing homes. Although as of the time this book goes to press it has not become wide-

spread or deep enough to take hold in the culture more broadly, these reactions are cause for hope.

278. Incidentally, a need for massive action in this regard is one reason why the religious practice of health care is so important to keep afloat in cultures where those who hold power are often hostile to religious freedom, especially in the practice of medicine. We need to continue to make sure we are in a position to mobilize and muster substantial aid, care, and hospitality should it come to that.

New City Press

New City Press is one of more than 20 publishing houses sponsored by the Focolare, a movement founded by Chiara Lubich to help bring about the realization of Jesus' prayer: "That all may be one" (John 17:21). In view of that goal, New City Press publishes books and resources that enrich the lives of people and help all to strive toward the unity of the entire human family. We are a member of the Association of Catholic Publishers.

www.newcitypress.com
202 Comforter Blvd.
Hyde Park, New York

Periodicals
Living City Magazine
www.livingcitymagazine.com

Scan to join our mailing list
for discounts and promotions
or go to www.newcitypress.com
and click on "join our email list."

This book is also available as an audio book.
Visit www.audible.com